BLUEPRINTS
The Junior Teacher's Resource Bank

Jim Fitzsimmons

Rhona Whiteford

Stanley Thornes (Publishers) Ltd

First published in 1994

First published in new binding in 1998 by:
Stanley Thornes (Publishers) Ltd

Reprinted in 2001 by:
Nelson Thornes Ltd
Delta Place
27 Bath Road
Cheltenham GL53 7TH
United Kingdom

01 02 03 04 05 / 10 9 8 7 6 5 4 3

A catalogue record for this book is available from the British Library.

ISBN 0–7487–3432–5

Typeset by Tech-Set, Gateshead, Tyne & Wear
Printed and bound in Great Britain by
Redwood Books, Trowbridge, Wiltshire

CONTENTS

INTRODUCTION

The *Blueprints Junior Teacher's Resource Bank* has been devised to provide a rich resource of photocopiable materials which you can use flexibly to meet a wide range of practical classroom needs.

It provides those basic materials that are used regularly in each area of the Junior curriculum. The emphasis is on Maths and English, but you will also find materials for Geography, History, Science, RE and topic work as well as material for organisational purposes and award stickers.

The aim of this resource is to provide you with materials that you can use, interpret and adapt creatively as you wish for a very wide range of personal needs. You will find suggestions for flexible use in the Teacher's Notes at the front. For example, the copymasters can be:

- used in classroom displays
- made into worksheets and creative writing sheets
- incorporated into letters and notices
- used with captions deleted as assessment sheets
- reduced or enlarged
- used as elements in posters.

A key feature is the very large ank of multi-purpose pictures which you can draw on freely to make up book covers, workcards and worksheets, games, use as elements in graphs and displays – and for a hundred other creative uses. They give you a huge topic-based resource of relevant pictures designed to save you hours of drawing time.

Written by experienced classroom practitioners, the material is specifically designed for Juniors in both content and appearance and will be an invaluable aid to the busy teacher.

TEACHER'S NOTES

Copymasters 1 and 2: Number lines 1 and 2

Copymaster 1 shows a series of number lines from 1 to 20 and Copymaster 2 shows a number line from 1 to 100. These lines can be cut up into strips which can either be mounted on card for the children to use or can be glued into the inside cover of a child's Maths book. The right-hand strips on Copymaster 1 are made up of centimetre squares and can be cut up to use for comparative measuring exercises.

Using Copymaster 2, each strip of 10 can be cut out and glued on card next to its consecutive strip to make a 100 line. The strips can be enlarged to use as a class display of the numbers 1 to 100.

Copymaster 3: 100 square 1 (blank)

The children can complete the square with numbers, colour in strips of 10 in separate colours, colour in multiplication patterns, or write the numerals for the multiplication patterns.

The grid can also be used for pattern drawing or for drawing symmetrical shapes, if a medial line is first drawn in a thicker black line, or coloured line. The grid can also be used to play 'Battleships' or as a grid on which to draw a simple map. For example, the children could draw a treasure island on the grid, then draw in horizontal and vertical axes. Using a separate sheet of paper they could write a secret message giving the grid references for five lots of buried treasure.

Copymaster 4: 100 square 2 (with numerals)

This can be enlarged to A3 size for wall display or reduced to A5 for inclusion in an exercise book. You can if you wish add questions to the square to make a work sheet. First copy the square at A5 size, cut this out as a block and glue it to the top of an A4 sheet of paper. You can now write questions in the space below this and then copy the quantity required.

Use the sheet for a 'fill in the missing numbers' exercise by blanking out random numbers or whole strips. You can also use the sheet to colour multiplication patterns, e.g. colour in every third square red. Patterns of numbers can be revealed by colouring in multiplication tables. For example, ask the children to colour in all the answers to the two times table and look at the pattern which emerges. Give the children several sheets and ask them to find the patterns made by the other multiplication tables.

Copymaster 5: Tens and units place value diagram

This sheet can be photocopied, reduced in size if necessary, and glued into the inside cover of individual Maths books or folders. The sheet can be made into a work sheet if desired by blanking out different sections for the children to fill in for themselves.

Copymasters 6 to 14: Multiplication tables

These sheets show the $\times 2$ to $\times 10$ multiplication tables. They can be displayed at A4 size on the wall or copied at the required size to make individual tables books.

The sheets show the commutative aspect of the tables and help the children to see the way in which the position of the numbers can be reversed and the answer remains the same.

Copymasters 15 to 17: Numerals 1 to 20 and Number words

These sheets show the numerals 1 to 20 and the corresponding number words. They can be enlarged for classroom display to give the children an easily accessible reference for the way numbers are written and also to help them with the spelling of the words.

Copymaster 18: Addition grid

This grid can be used for adding up to 20. The children can fill in the squares by starting at the top of the vertical axis and adding each of the numbers shown on the horizontal axis as they fill in each square across, e.g. 0 plus 0 equals 0, then 0 plus 1 equals 1. When they have completed the first row, they move down the vertical axis to the row beginning with number 1 and repeat the process until each row is filled. When the table is complete and checked it can be used as a quick reference for simple addition and will also give useful practice in reading coordinates.

Copymaster 19: Subtraction grid

This grid can be used for subtraction of numbers up to 20. As with the previous sheet, the children should start at the top of the vertical axis and subtract each of the numbers on the horizontal axis from that number to fill in the first row. They should then work down the vertical axis, repeating the process for each row until the grid is filled.

Copymaster 20: Multiplication grid

Use this grid to give practice in multiplication tables. To fill in the grid, the children should start at the top of the vertical axis and multiply by each of the numbers on the horizontal axis. They should write each answer in the square underneath the number they have multiplied by, to fill in the top row. They should then repeat this process along each row to fill in the grid.

Copymasters 21 to 23: Squared paper 1 to 3

These sheets provide grids of $1\,cm^2$, $2\,cm^2$ and $5\,cm^2$. Use them for symmetrical drawings, work on area and as graph paper.

Copymaster 24: Conversion charts and symbols
This shows the common units of measurement for weight, length, capacity and time, plus a list of mathematical symbols and abbreviations. It can be enlarged for classroom display, or reduced for inclusion in individual Maths books or folders.

Copymasters 25 and 26: Shapes 1 and 2
Copymaster 25 shows the common 2D shapes, while common 3D shapes are illustrated on Copymaster 26. These sheets can be enlarged for classroom display to give a ready reference chart to help the children to recognise and name the basic shapes encountered at this level. If required the sheets can also be reduced for inclusion in individual Maths books or folders.

Copymasters 27 to 33: 3D nets 1 to 7
Copies of these sheets can be used to make 3D models of some of the shapes shown on Copymaster 26. They can be enlarged or reduced as required and to make stronger models the copies can be stuck on to card. The children can decorate each of the surfaces with their own designs and the models make attractive mobiles when hung from the classroom ceiling.

Copymaster 34: Clocks 1
This shows a large smiling clock face with separate hands. This sheet can be glued on to card and then cut out by the children to make individual teaching clocks. The hands can be fixed on to the clock using a brass paper fastener. (The children may need assistance with fixing on the hands.)

Copymaster 35: Clocks 2
This shows a series of clock faces with numerals but no hands. You can add hands and ask the children to write in the time below each clock. Alternatively, write the times and ask the children to draw in the hands. The sheet can be enlarged to A3, and examples of the main times (e.g. o'clock, half past, quarter past, quarter to etc.) can be drawn and written in for reference.

Copymaster 36: Clocks 3
This shows a series of blank clock faces. It can be used in the same way as Copymaster 35 but this time the children have to draw in their own numerals. This will help them to remember the position of the numbers on the clock face.

Copymaster 37: Clocks 4
This shows a series of blank digital clocks. It can be used to give practice in making the connection between the different representations of the time. Use a large teaching clock to show the time in the traditional way and ask the children to draw in the time as it would be shown on a digital clock. Alternatively, write the time underneath the digital clocks in words and ask the children to write in the numerals on the clocks.

Copymasters 38 and 39: Days of the week and Months of the year
These sheets can be reduced to A5 to include in children's dictionaries or exercise books, or enlarged for wall display as part of the classroom vocabulary bank. They can be made into worksheets by blanking out all but the initial letters of the words. The children can then be asked to complete the lists by making reference to the classroom display.

Copymasters 40 to 43: Seasons 1 to 4
The children can make their own contributions to these pictures by adding animals, vehicles or people in connection with seasonal topic work. These sheets can also be used to write poetry, reportive writing, vocabulary or imaginative stories on. They could also be enlarged for classroom display as part of a topic on 'Time'.

Copymasters 44 and 45: Ruled handwriting sheets 1 and 2
Use these when individual sheets of paper are needed for a special piece of writing. For hand writing practice on ascenders and descenders use Copymaster 45 which has a dashed mid line for guidance.

Copymaster 46: Music staves
This sheet can be copied and used as it is or cut up into strips for writing out simple phrases for the children. The strips should be mounted on card for ease of use.

Copymaster 47: Book report
The children can fill in this sheet after reading a book to record their impressions of the experience.

Copymaster 48: Books I have read
This can be used as an individual reading record filled in by the child, or as part of the record keeping for a paired reading scheme. It can also be used as a record of home or library reading.

Copymaster 49: Reading record
This can be used to record the books read by a child, the date and any comments which may be necessary. It can be used as part of the teacher's class record, as an aid to assessment and a way to monitor progress. It could also be used as part of a paired reading scheme where the child and parent would be invited to make comments on their own reading practice at home.

Copymaster 50: Reading award
Duplicate a small quantity of these to give out as rewards for good effort in reading.

Copymasters 51 and 52: Characters from fiction and legend 1 and 2
Use these sheets enlarged as part of the classroom display or library area, to stimulate interest in the characters and try to encourage the children to become familiar with their exploits by looking for books containing stories about them. Alternatively, you could make individual sheets for each of the characters by photocopying the sheet once, cutting out the pictures and glueing them on to separate sheets. Add any extra writing you wish, then photocopy them as required. Individual pictures could also be enlarged to A3 size for wall display.

Copymaster 53: Fantasy characters
This sheet could be used in the same way as suggested for Copymasters 51 and 52. In addition, the children could be given copies of the whole sheet and asked to make up a story containing several of the characters shown.

Copymasters 54 to 57: Story titles 1 to 4
These sheets can be used in many ways. You could enlarge one sheet for classroom discussion and write on it vocabulary, different story titles on the theme, story plans or types of characters. The sheets can also be used for poems, handwriting or topic work. They could also be used for the children to write imaginative lists of equipment they might need in order to conquer the aliens or explore the valley of the dinosaurs.

Copymaster 58: Crossword blank
Use this sheet to make simple crosswords. Decide on your clues and try to fit the words inside the grid. It is not necessary to use the entire grid as any squares which are not needed can be shaded in. The large grid gives scope for making the crossword as hard or as easy as you think necessary. More able children could try to create their own crosswords.

Copymasters 59 and 60: Phonic checklists 1 and 2
Copymaster 59 shows the common consonant combinations and digraphs, while Copymaster 60 shows the common vowel combinations and digraphs. They can be used by you as a sounds recognition record for each child. They can be reduced to A5 for inclusion in the children's English exercise books, folders or dictionaries, or can be enlarged for use as posters. You can make a phonic game by cutting out the individual sound combinations, glueing each sound on to a separate sheet of A4 paper and giving one each to groups of three children. The children can have a set time to think of ten or twenty words which begin with or contain that sound.

Copymaster 61: Christmas pictures 1 (secular)
Each picture can be enlarged to A4 size and used as a sheet on which to write greetings, lists, notices, poems, stories and letters connected with Christmas. The pictures can also be used as a base for cards, calendars and posters of Christmas events, or they can be coloured to make a border around seasonal work.

Copymaster 62: Christmas pictures 2 (religious)
Use this in the same way as Copymaster 61. In addition, the pictures can be cut out, mounted on card and, with a small card prop at the back, used as figures in a 3D stable scene. You can make a simple stable from a small shoe box. The figures can also be made into simple puppets for the telling of the Christmas story by glueing them on to card and fixing a plastic straw horizontally to the base of the figure for use as a handle. To make a composite stable picture for the top of a story sheet, copy the sheet once, cut out the figures and then arrange them on a separate sheet, overlapping some to fit them on, and enclose the figures in a stable outline.

Copymaster 63: Easter pictures 1 (secular)
Use this in the same way as Copymaster 61, but you can also use these pictures for general topic work on Spring. Enlarge single pictures to A4 size and write in vocabulary, phonic word lists or titles of topics. For example, you could write in 'Spring' alongside an enlarged picture of the Spring flowers.

Copymaster 64: Easter pictures 2 (religious)
Use this in the same way as Copymaster 61. Church schools might like to copy a single motif at the top of a page to use as a letter heading for notices about religious events.

Copymasters 65 to 67: Symbols of religious faiths 1 to 3
These religious symbols and motifs can be used as appropriate headings on letters about religious events or on posters and notices around the school. They can also be used at times of religious festivals for reportive writing or as designs for cards.

Copymaster 68: Weather chart
This sheet can be adapted to keep a record of the weather for a week, a month or a term. Copies of the weather symbols can be cut out and stuck on to the daily squares on the monthly record or the children can draw in the symbols. Different groups of children can be encouraged to keep the weather record each month and a picture of the weather can be built up over a whole year by the members of the class. The recorded information can be shown on graphs, tables or charts.

Copymasters 69 to 107: Topic pictures
The topics covered are: sea and land creatures, dinosaurs, fossils, parts of a flower, the human skeleton, the digestive system, the ear, the eye, animals and their young, animal homes, the life cycles of a butterfly, a frog and a human, Earth in space, generating electricity, how a steam engine works, motorcycle and bicycle, space vehicles, bridges, food chains, landforms, habitats, types of transport, the water cycle, common trees and their leaves, garden and wild flowers, farm animals, types of food and the orchestra. The illustrations could be copied individually on to a sheet and enlarged for wall display, or for use as topic covers. Vocabulary could be written beneath the pictures, or one picture could be enlarged and a crossword drawn inside it. The pictures could be copied or traced by the children. Alternatively, provide copies of the outlines and ask the children to add colour and texture.

You could make posters or work cards for specific teaching points, e.g. endangered animals, sets of animals from specific habitats, use of camouflage, carnivorous and herbivorous animals, land and sea animals, groups of trees and flowers. To do this, copy one sheet, cut out the pictures required and glue them in the desired arrangement on a separate sheet, add any writing or instructions and use this composite sheet as your master copy.

Use the sheets as a base for art work in connection with your topic. For example, you could show the children how to compose different habitat backgrounds using a variety of media (chalk, paint, felt pens, fabric, wax crayon, wax rubbings and paper collage), then colour the appropriate animal pictures, cut them out and stick them on to the finished backgrounds.

Copymaster 108: Compass points
This can be reduced for individual reference, or enlarged as part of any classroom display involving the use of direction.

Copymasters 109 to 115: Maps 1 to 7
The maps provided are of the British Isles, England, Ireland, Scotland, Wales, Europe and the world. They can be used for recording information such as locations of towns and cities, differences in land use or land type, historical boundaries or invasions. They can be made into individual worksheets to suit your class needs, or enlarged to provide information within a class display.

The flags on Copymasters 109 to 113 can be enlarged and used as topic covers for topics on the individual countries, or they can be used as integral parts of a class display on the British Isles or any of the individual countries. They can also be used for displays on the various patron saints days of the different countries. This can lead to a discussion of the composition of the Union Jack and the identification of the different flags within it.

Copymasters 116 and 117: Famous buildings 1 and 2
These sheets can be used to create individual work sheets for topic work on buildings. They can also be enlarged to make illustrations for class display.

Copymaster 118: Family tree
This can be used to gather information for a topic on 'My family', or simply as a way for the children to find out about their own family history. Remember when carrying out any research of this kind to be sensitive and aware of such situations as adoption, single parent families and divorce.

Copymaster 119: The royal family
This is a simple family tree of the present queen's immediate family. It can be used as a starting point for a topic on 'The Royal Family' or as a cover sheet for such a topic. By cutting out the individual illustrations you can make separate sheets for writing about the different members of the family.

Copymasters 120 to 125: Then and now 1 to 6
Copymaster 120 shows the development of four common household items during the last fifty years. The illustrations can be used as reference points for topics on 'The Home' or 'Machinery'. They can be made into individual work sheets where the children are asked to find information about the objects, or they can be used as a sorting exercise whereby the pictures are cut out from the sheet and the children have to take each set of items and place them in chronological order, or take the whole set of pictures and group all the 1940 objects together, then all the 1970 objects together, and finally all the 1990 objects.

Copymasters 121, 122, 123 and 124 cover transport by air, sea and rail and cars through the ages. Use these pictures as described above and also for inclusion in topics such as 'Transport', 'Machinery', 'Cars', 'Trains' and 'Things that go'.

Copymaster 125 shows families dressed in clothes typical of the 1940s, 1960s and 1990s. These illustrations can be enlarged for use in a class display, or used as separate pictures to illustrate topics on 'Clothes', 'Costume' and 'Fashion'. They could also be used as part of an investigation into the way people lived during a certain period, e.g. 'The War Years', 'The Swinging Sixties', or 'Life Today'.

Copymasters 126 to 129: Homes and toys time lines
Copymasters 126 and 127 show the development of homes through the ages and can be used as part of a topic on 'Homes and houses'. The sheets can be enlarged for class display, cut up and re-pasted to form a single continuous line. As described previously, the individual illustrations can also be cut out to make separate worksheets. The toys time line on Copymasters 128 and 129 can be used in the same way to link with topics on 'Childhood', or 'Toys and pastimes'.

Copymasters 130 and 131: Famous people in history
These illustrations can be used in the same ways as mentioned previously and can be included in topics on the single famous individual, or as a topic on 'Famous people' generally.

Copymasters 132 to 142: Historical pictures
Use these as reference material enlarged for classroom use to make comparisons between different historical periods.

Copymaster 143: Teacher's note heading
Use this for essential short messages to be sent home, such as arrangements for cooking, swimming or regular outings. For longer messages, or to choose the illustration you prefer, simply copy one sheet, cut off the version you do not need, enlarge the remaining version to the required size and photocopy as required. Keep one as a master copy for future occasions.

Copymaster 144: Special event letter heading
As indicated by its title, this letter heading should be used sparingly during the year for letters to parents about such things as sponsored events, performances, meetings or demonstrations. Copy one sheet and type in your letter, then copy as required.

Copymasters 145 to 150: Special awards and award certificates 1 to 5
Use these as special rewards as required, in each of the different curriculum subjects. Included are four special awards, a class award, and a super worker award for those occasions where a general award needs to be made without reference to a particular subject or where a particular subject is not covered by the other certificates.

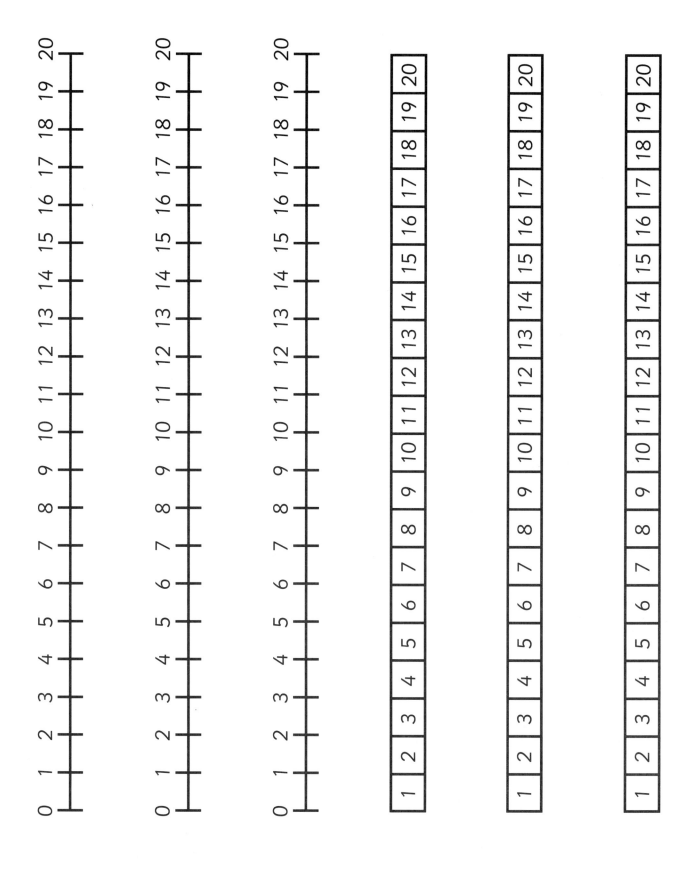

1	2	3	4	5	6	7	8	9	10

11	12	13	14	15	16	17	18	19	20

21	22	23	24	25	26	27	28	29	30

31	32	33	34	35	36	37	38	39	40

41	42	43	44	45	46	47	48	49	50

51	52	53	54	55	56	57	58	59	60

61	62	63	64	65	66	67	68	69	70

71	72	73	74	75	76	77	78	79	80

81	82	83	84	85	86	87	88	89	90

91	92	93	94	95	96	97	98	99	100

100 square 1

100 square 2

1	2	3	4	5	6	7	8	9	10
11	12	13	14	15	16	17	18	19	20
21	22	23	24	25	26	27	28	29	30
31	32	33	34	35	36	37	38	39	40
41	42	43	44	45	46	47	48	49	50
51	52	53	54	55	56	57	58	59	60
61	62	63	64	65	66	67	68	69	70
71	72	73	74	75	76	77	78	79	80
81	82	83	84	85	86	87	88	89	90
91	92	93	94	95	96	97	98	99	100

Tens and units

‖‖‖‖‖	one ten	=	10
‖‖‖‖‖ │	one ten and one unit	=	11
‖‖‖‖‖ ││	one ten and two units	=	12
‖‖‖‖‖ │││	one ten and three units	=	13
‖‖‖‖‖ ││││	one ten and four units	=	14
‖‖‖‖‖ │││││	one ten and five units	=	15
‖‖‖‖‖ ││││││	one ten and six units	=	16
‖‖‖‖‖ │││││││	one ten and seven units	=	17
‖‖‖‖‖ ││││││││	one ten and eight units	=	18
‖‖‖‖‖ │││││││││	one ten and nine units	=	19
‖‖‖‖‖ ‖‖‖‖‖	two tens	=	20

2 × Tables

2 × 1 = 2	1 × 2 = 2
2 × 2 = 4	2 × 2 = 4
2 × 3 = 6	3 × 2 = 6
2 × 4 = 8	4 × 2 = 8
2 × 5 = 10	5 × 2 = 10
2 × 6 = 12	6 × 2 = 12
2 × 7 = 14	7 × 2 = 14
2 × 8 = 16	8 × 2 = 16
2 × 9 = 18	9 × 2 = 18
2 × 10 = 20	10 × 2 = 20
2 × 11 = 22	11 × 2 = 22
2 × 12 = 24	12 × 2 = 24

3 × Tables

$3 \times 1 = 3$ $1 \times 3 = 3$

$3 \times 2 = 6$ $2 \times 3 = 6$

$3 \times 3 = 9$ $3 \times 3 = 9$

$3 \times 4 = 12$ $4 \times 3 = 12$

$3 \times 5 = 15$ $5 \times 3 = 15$

$3 \times 6 = 18$ $6 \times 3 = 18$

$3 \times 7 = 21$ $7 \times 3 = 21$

$3 \times 8 = 24$ $8 \times 3 = 24$

$3 \times 9 = 27$ $9 \times 3 = 27$

$3 \times 10 = 30$ $10 \times 3 = 30$

$3 \times 11 = 33$ $11 \times 3 = 33$

$3 \times 12 = 36$ $12 \times 3 = 36$

4 × Tables

4 × 1 = 4	1 × 4 = 4
4 × 2 = 8	2 × 4 = 8
4 × 3 = 12	3 × 4 = 12
4 × 4 = 16	4 × 4 = 16
4 × 5 = 20	5 × 4 = 20
4 × 6 = 24	6 × 4 = 24
4 × 7 = 28	7 × 4 = 28
4 × 8 = 32	8 × 4 = 32
4 × 9 = 36	9 × 4 = 36
4 × 10 = 40	10 × 4 = 40
4 × 11 = 44	11 × 4 = 44
4 × 12 = 48	12 × 4 = 48

5 × Tables

5 × 1 = 5	1 × 5 = 5
5 × 2 = 10	2 × 5 = 10
5 × 3 = 15	3 × 5 = 15
5 × 4 = 20	4 × 5 = 20
5 × 5 = 25	5 × 5 = 25
5 × 6 = 30	6 × 5 = 30
5 × 7 = 35	7 × 5 = 35
5 × 8 = 40	8 × 5 = 40
5 × 9 = 45	9 × 5 = 45
5 × 10 = 50	10 × 5 = 50
5 × 11 = 55	11 × 5 = 55
5 × 12 = 60	12 × 5 = 60

6 × Tables

6 × 1 = 6	1 × 6 = 6
6 × 2 = 12	2 × 6 = 12
6 × 3 = 18	3 × 6 = 18
6 × 4 = 24	4 × 6 = 24
6 × 5 = 30	5 × 6 = 30
6 × 6 = 36	6 × 6 = 36
6 × 7 = 42	7 × 6 = 42
6 × 8 = 48	8 × 6 = 48
6 × 9 = 54	9 × 6 = 54
6 × 10 = 60	10 × 6 = 60
6 × 11 = 66	11 × 6 = 66
6 × 12 = 72	12 × 6 = 72

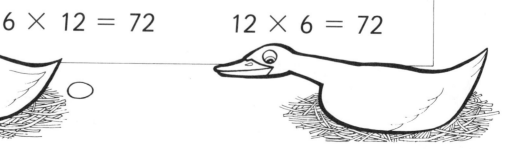

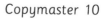

7 × Tables

7 × 1 = 7	1 × 7 = 7
7 × 2 = 14	2 × 7 = 14
7 × 3 = 21	3 × 7 = 21
7 × 4 = 28	4 × 7 = 28
7 × 5 = 35	5 × 7 = 35
7 × 6 = 42	6 × 7 = 42
7 × 7 = 49	7 × 7 = 49
7 × 8 = 56	8 × 7 = 56
7 × 9 = 63	9 × 7 = 63
7 × 10 = 70	10 × 7 = 70
7 × 11 = 77	11 × 7 = 77
7 × 12 = 84	12 × 7 = 84

8 × Tables

8 × 1 = 8	1 × 8 = 8
8 × 2 = 16	2 × 8 = 16
8 × 3 = 24	3 × 8 = 24
8 × 4 = 32	4 × 8 = 32
8 × 5 = 40	5 × 8 = 40
8 × 6 = 48	6 × 8 = 48
8 × 7 = 56	7 × 8 = 56
8 × 8 = 64	8 × 8 = 64
8 × 9 = 72	9 × 8 = 72
8 × 10 = 80	10 × 8 = 80
8 × 11 = 88	11 × 8 = 88
8 × 12 = 96	12 × 8 = 96

9 × Tables

9 × 1 = 9	1 × 9 = 9
9 × 2 = 18	2 × 9 = 18
9 × 3 = 27	3 × 9 = 27
9 × 4 = 36	4 × 9 = 36
9 × 5 = 45	5 × 9 = 45
9 × 6 = 54	6 × 9 = 54
9 × 7 = 63	7 × 9 = 63
9 × 8 = 72	8 × 9 = 72
9 × 9 = 81	9 × 9 = 81
9 × 10 = 90	10 × 9 = 90
9 × 11 = 99	11 × 9 = 99
9 × 12 = 108	12 × 9 = 108

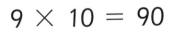

10 × Tables

10 × 1 = 10	1 × 10 = 10
10 × 2 = 20	2 × 10 = 20
10 × 3 = 30	3 × 10 = 30
10 × 4 = 40	4 × 10 = 40
10 × 5 = 50	5 × 10 = 50
10 × 6 = 60	6 × 10 = 60
10 × 7 = 70	7 × 10 = 70
10 × 8 = 80	8 × 10 = 80
10 × 9 = 90	9 × 10 = 90
10 × 10 = 100	10 × 10 = 100
10 × 11 = 110	11 × 10 = 110
10 × 12 = 120	12 × 10 = 120

1	2
3	4
5	6
7	8
9	10

11	12
13	14
15	16
17	18
19	20

one	two
three	four
five	six
seven	eight
nine	ten
eleven	twelve
thirteen	fourteen
fifteen	sixteen
seventeen	eighteen
nineteen	twenty

Addition Grid

+	0	1	2	3	4	5	6	7	8	9	10
0	0	1									
1											
2											
3											
4											
5											
6											
7											
8											
9											
10											

Subtraction Grid

−	0	1	2	3	4	5	6	7	8	9	10
20											
19											
18											
17											
16											
15											
14											
13											
12											
11											
10											
9											X
8										X	X
7									X	X	X
6								X	X	X	X
5							X	X	X	X	X
4						X	X	X	X	X	X
3				X	X	X	X	X	X	X	X
2			X	X	X	X	X	X	X	X	X
1			X	X	X	X	X	X	X	X	X

Multiplication Grid

0	1	2	3	4	5	6	7	8	9	10
1										
2										
3										
4										
5										
6										
7										
8										
9										
10										

Weight

mg 1000 milligrams = 1 gram
g 1000 grams = 1 kilogram
kg 100 kilograms = 1 quintal
10 quintals = 1 tonne

Imperial equivalents

1 g = 0.035 ounces
1 kg = 2.21 pounds
1 tonne = 0.98 tons

Length

mm 10 millimetres = 1 centimetre
cm 10 centimetres = 1 decimetre
dm 10 decimetres = 1 metre
m 1000 metres = 1 kilometre km
1 metre = 1000 mm
100 cm
10 dm

Imperial equivalents

1 inch = 2.54 cm
1 yd = 0.91 m
1 m = 1.09 yd
1 km = 0.62 miles

Capacity

ml 10 millilitres = 1 centilitre
cl 10 centilitres = 1 decilitre
dl 10 decilitres = 1 litre
l 10 litres = 1 decalitre
100 litres = 1 hectolitre hl

Imperial equivalents

1 pint = 568 ml
1 pint = 20 fluid oz
1 gallon = 4.546 litres
1 litre = 1.759 pints

Signs, symbols and abbreviations

=	is equal to	∈	is a member of the set of
≠	is not equal to		
≐	is approx. equal to	∉	is not a member of the set of
≡	is identical to	cm	centimetres
		mm	millimetres
≯	not greater than	m	metres
		km	kilometres
>	greater than	g	grams
<	less than	kg	kilograms
≮	not less than	ml	millilitres
Σ	the sum of	cl	centilitres
∠	angle	∴	therefore
∞	infinity	∵	because

Time

60 seconds = 1 minute
60 minutes = 1 hour
24 hours = 1 day
7 days = 1 week
4 weeks = 1 month
12 months = 1 year
365 days = 1 year
366 days = 1 leap year
10 years = 1 decade
100 years = 1 century
1000 years = 1 millennium

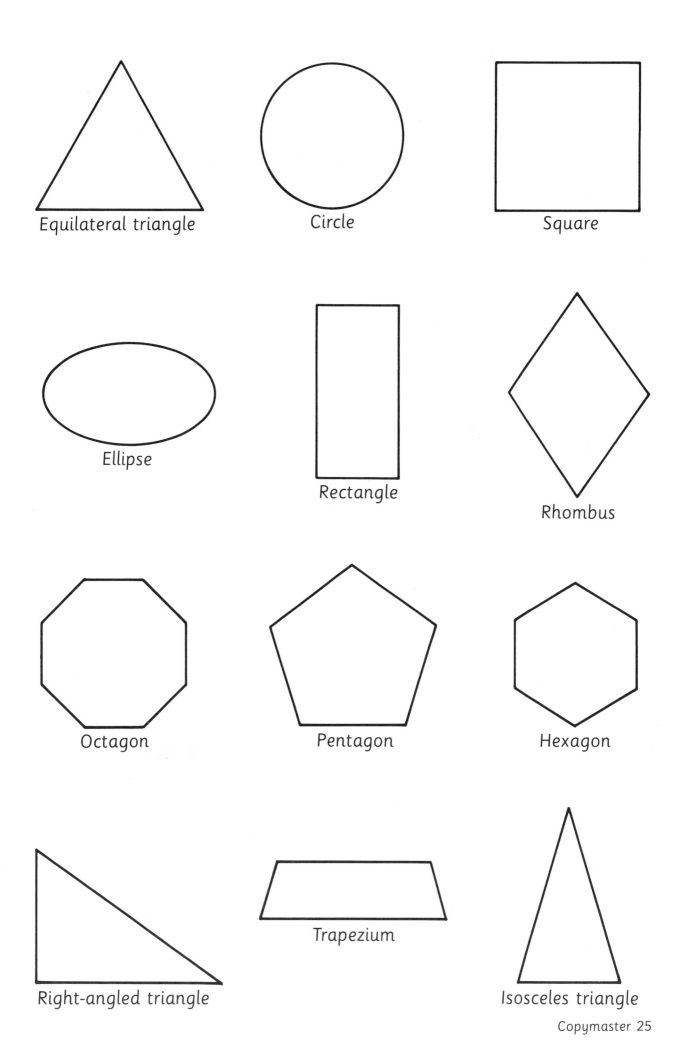

Equilateral triangle

Circle

Square

Ellipse

Rectangle

Rhombus

Octagon

Pentagon

Hexagon

Right-angled triangle

Trapezium

Isosceles triangle

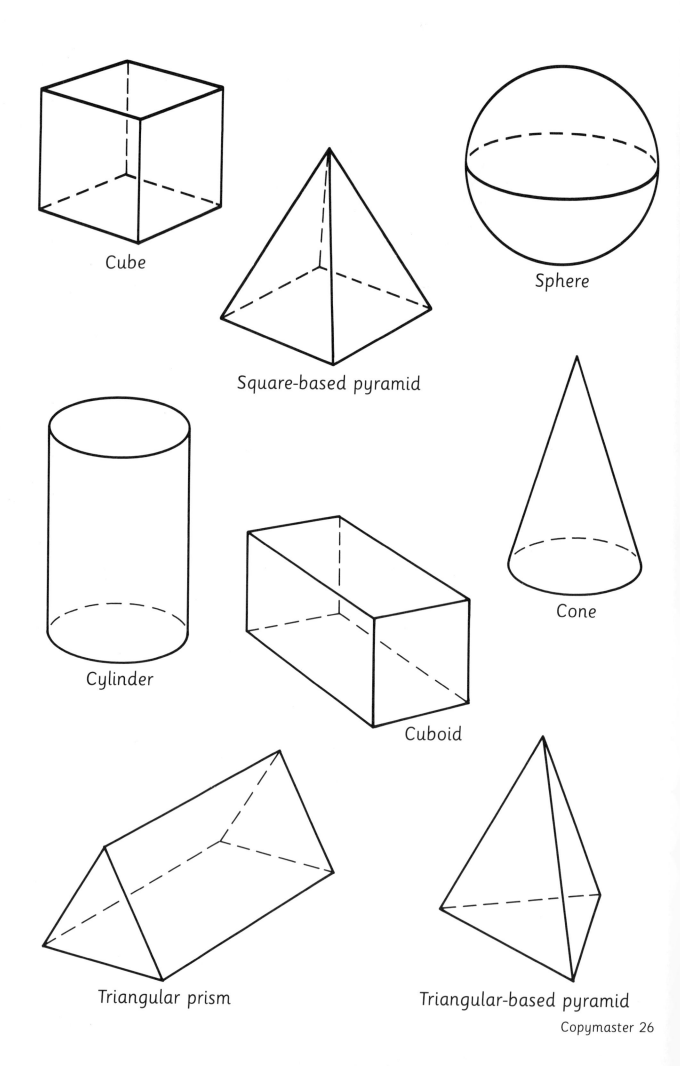

Cube

Square-based pyramid

Sphere

Cylinder

Cuboid

Cone

Triangular prism

Triangular-based pyramid

Cube

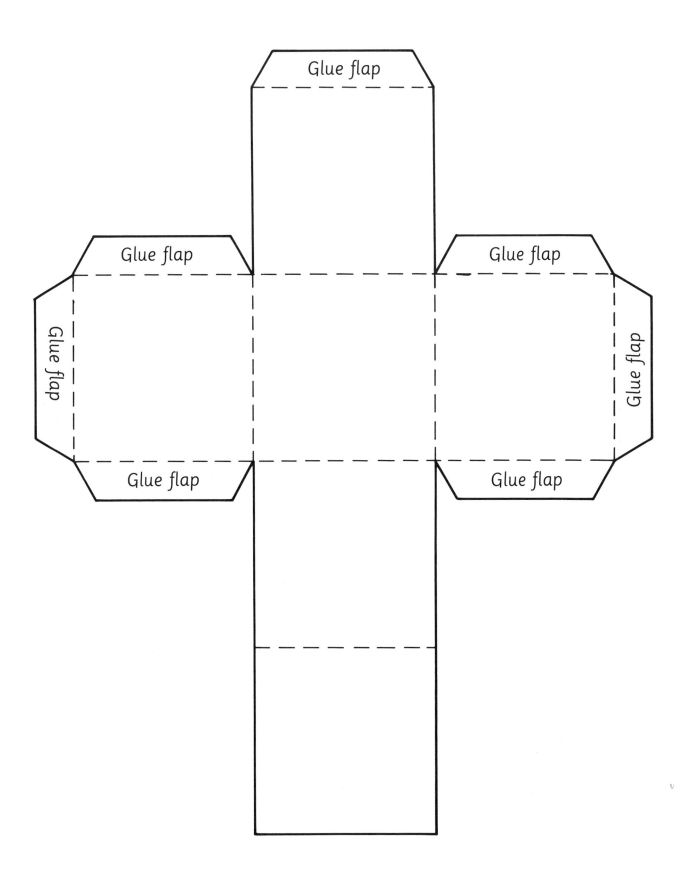

Cuboid

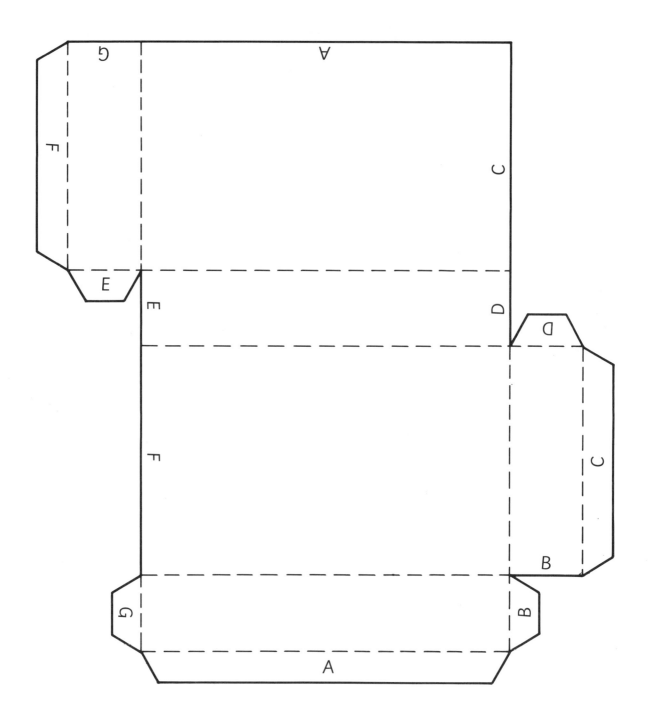

Fold along the dotted lines and glue the marked flaps to the corresponding marked edges.

Square-based pyramid

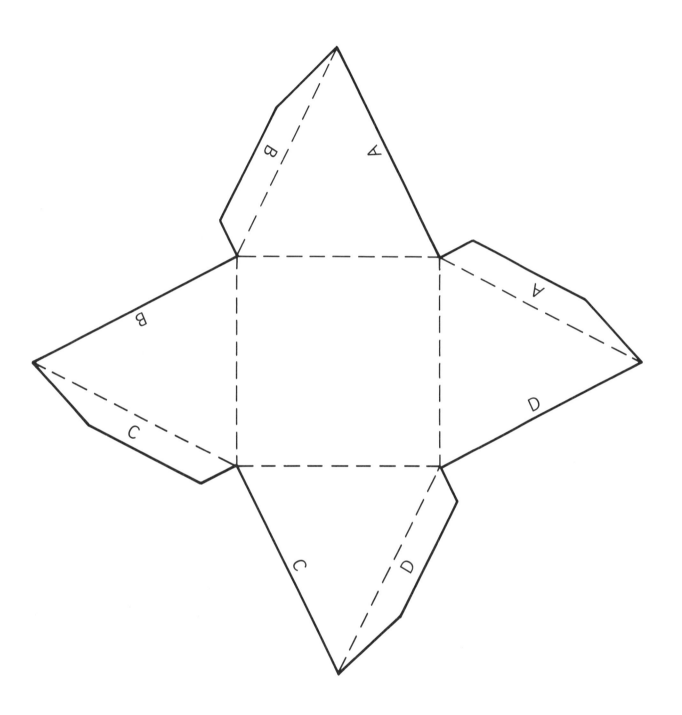

Fold along the dotted lines and glue the marked flaps to the corresponding marked edges.

Triangular prism

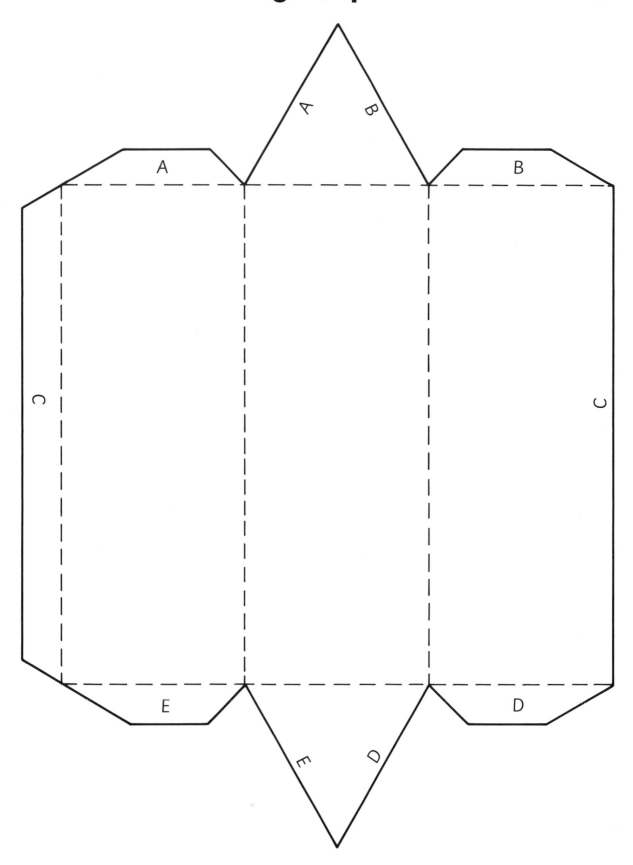

Fold along the dotted lines and glue the marked flaps to the corresponding marked edges.

Tetrahedron

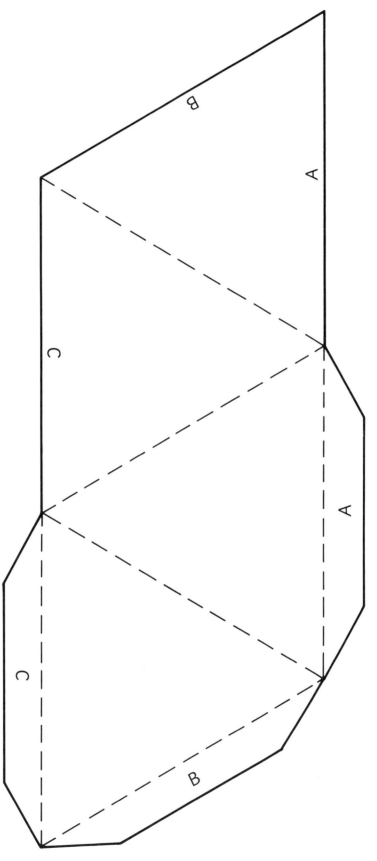

Fold along the dotted lines and glue the marked flaps to the corresponding marked edges.

Dodecahedron

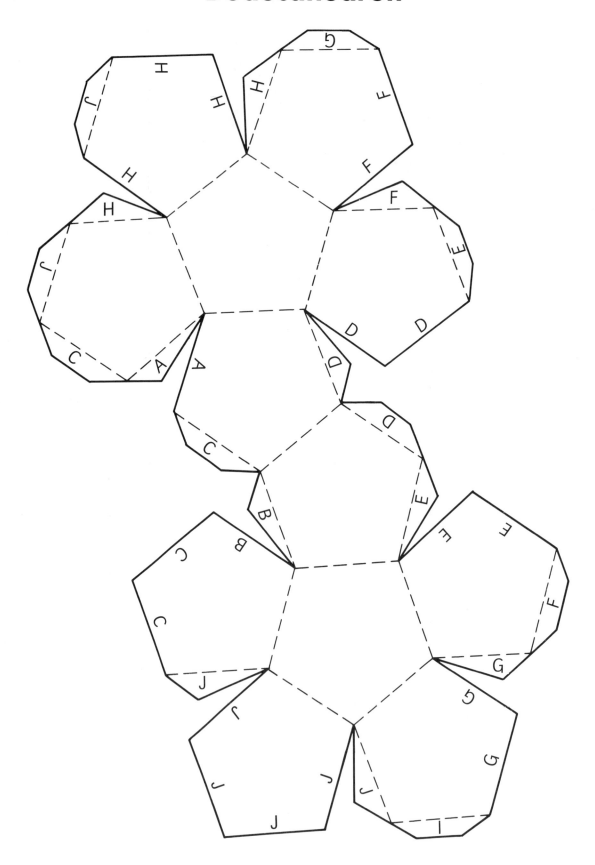

Fold along the dotted lines and glue the marked flaps to the corresponding marked edges.

Icosahedron

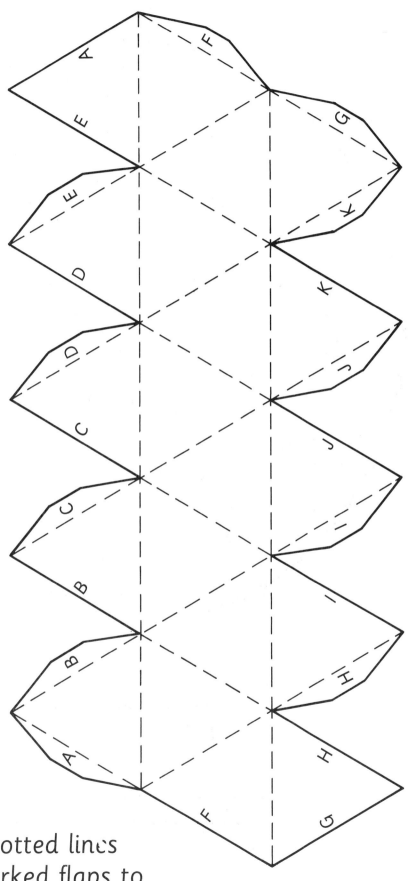

Fold along the dotted lines
and glue the marked flaps to
the corresponding marked edges.

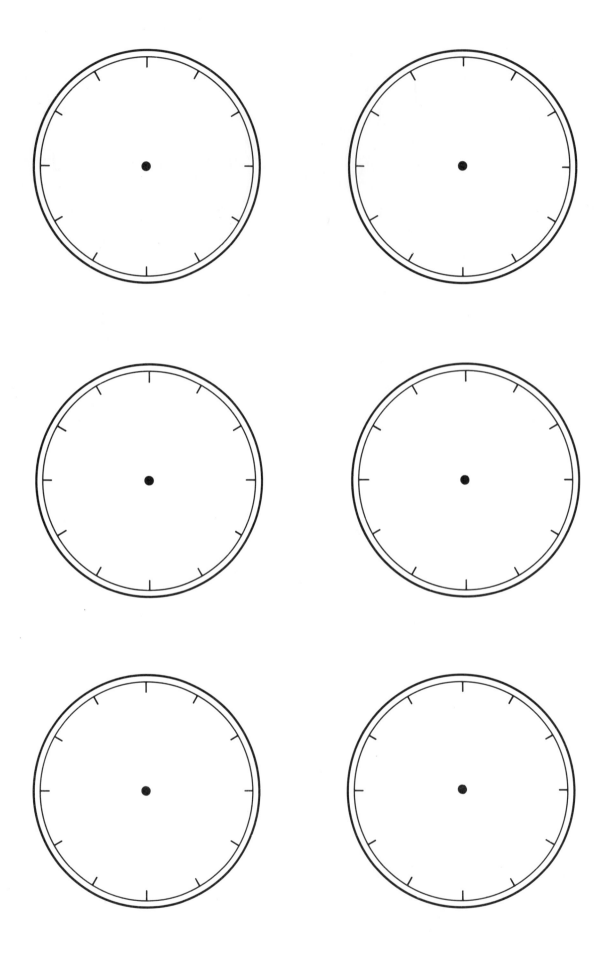

Days of the week

Sunday
Monday
Tuesday
Wednesday
Thursday
Friday
Saturday

Months of the year

January	February
March	April
May	June
July	August
September	October
November	December

Spring

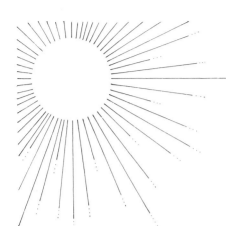

Summer

Autumn

Winter

Handwriting sheet 1

Handwriting sheet 2

Music staves

Book report

Name of book: _____

Author: _____

Summary of book: _____

_____

_____

_____

_____

_____

What I liked most: _____

_____

_____

What I did not like: _____

_____

_____

Books I have read

I have read these books this month:

Title of book	Author	Date finished

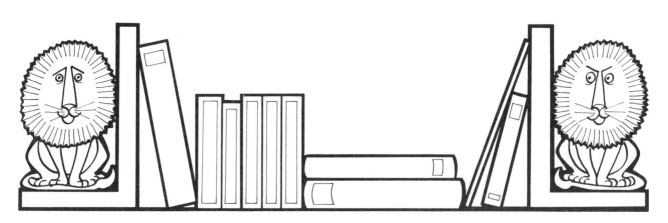

Reading record

Name: _____

Date	Book	Comment

Reading award

Awarded to

_____

for

_____

_____

_____

Signed

_____

Date

_____

Robin Hood and Maid Marion

Long John Silver

Scrooge

Robinson Crusoe

King Arthur

St George

William Tell

Ulysses

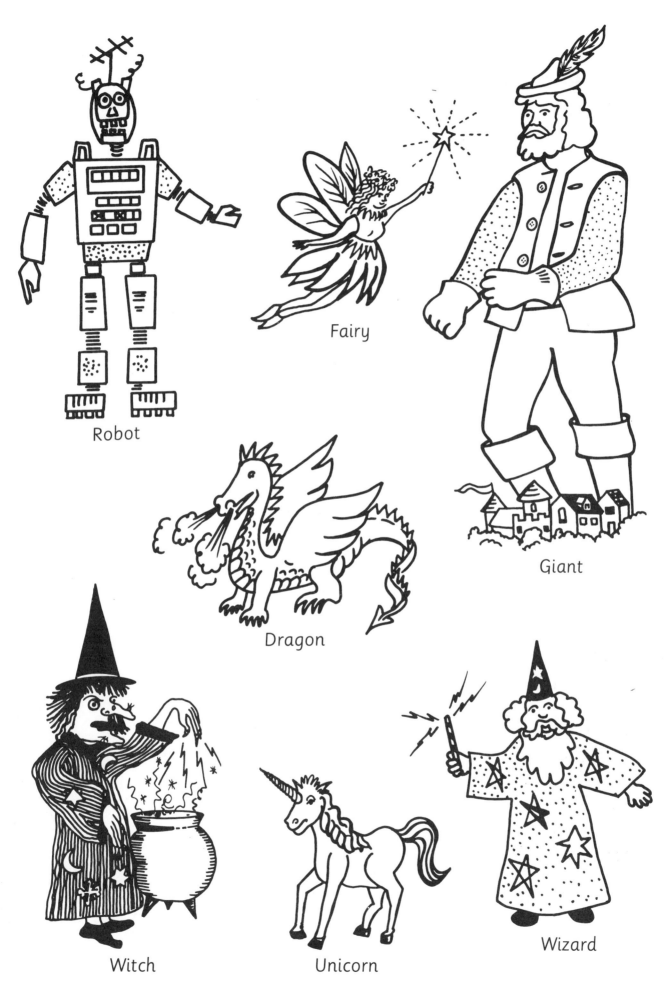

Robot

Fairy

Giant

Dragon

Witch

Unicorn

Wizard

COMPUTER ADVENTURE

Valley of the Dinosaurs

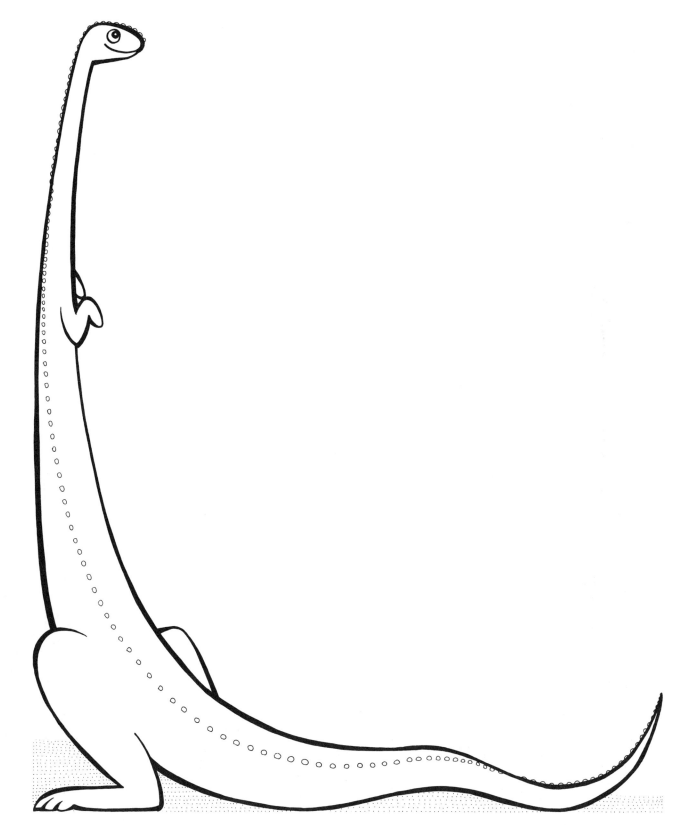

ALIEN

Mystery adventure

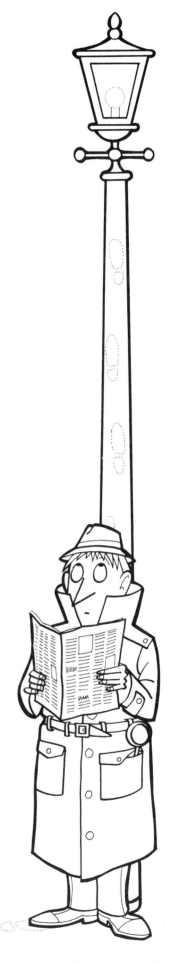

Crossword blank

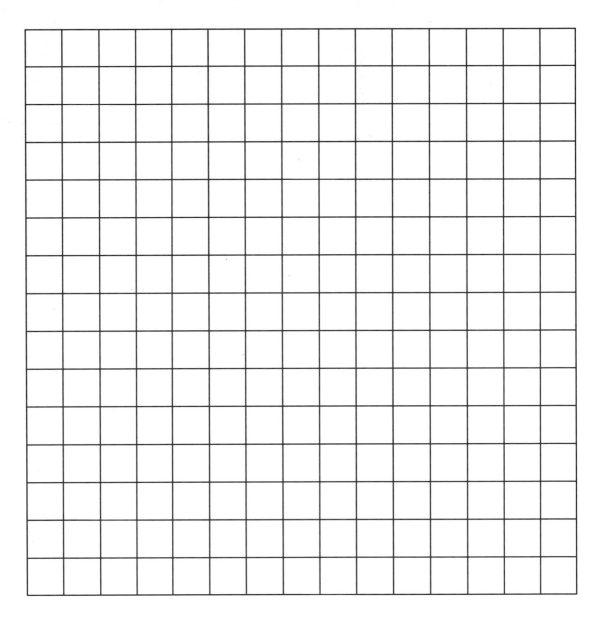

Clues across

_____
_____
_____
_____
_____
_____
_____
_____

Clues down

_____
_____
_____
_____
_____
_____
_____
_____

Phonic checklist 1

bl	fl	cl	gl
pl	sl	sc	sm
sp	sk	sw	st
gr	cr	dr	tr
nd	nt	nk	st
sk	mp	ck	ll
ff	ss	th	ch
sh	kn	ph	qu

Phonic checklist 2

ee	oo	ea (as in h<u>ea</u>d)	ea (as in n<u>ea</u>t)
ow (as in d<u>ow</u>n)	ow (as in sn<u>ow</u>)	oa	oi
oy	ou	ay	ai
a–e	o–e	i–e	u–e
er	aw	or	ear
ir	ar	ie	ur
ui	au	ew	

Calvary

Palm branch

Crown of thorns
with nails

Paschal
candle

Risen Christ

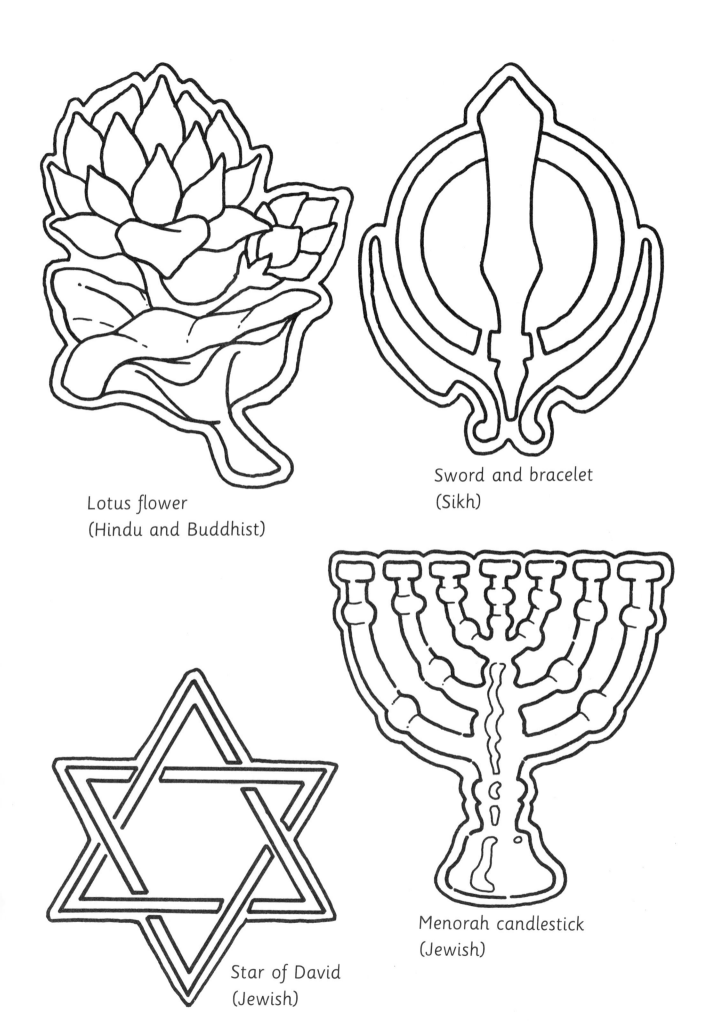

Lotus flower
(Hindu and Buddhist)

Sword and bracelet
(Sikh)

Menorah candlestick
(Jewish)

Star of David
(Jewish)

Shiva
(Hindu God)

Mahayana
(Buddhist wheel)

The Buddha

Cross
(Christian)

Crescent and star
(Islam)

Dove of peace
(Christian)

Weather chart

Sunny   Cloudy   Windy   Foggy   Hail   Rain   Snow

Month: _____

Sunday	Monday	Tuesday	Wednesday	Thursday	Friday	Saturday

Crab

Clownfish

Dolphin

Jellyfish

Eel

Flying fish

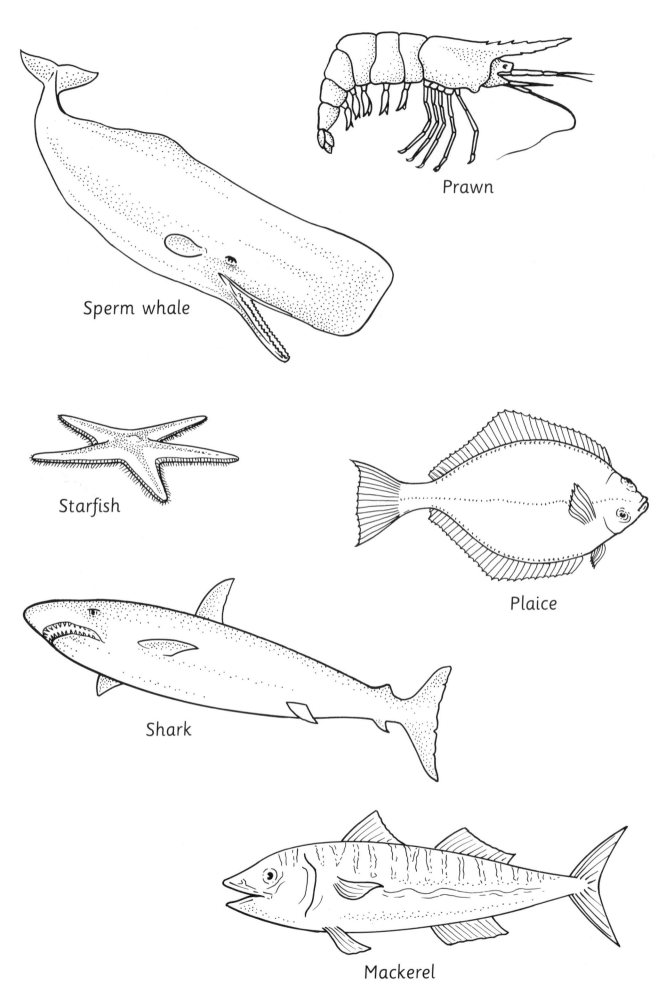

Prawn

Sperm whale

Starfish

Plaice

Shark

Mackerel

Octopus

Sea horse

Turtle

Ray

Sturgeon

Elephant

Giraffe

Lion

Tiger

Hippopotamus

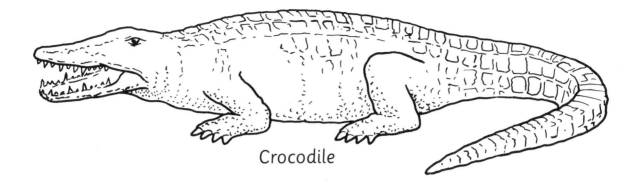

Crocodile

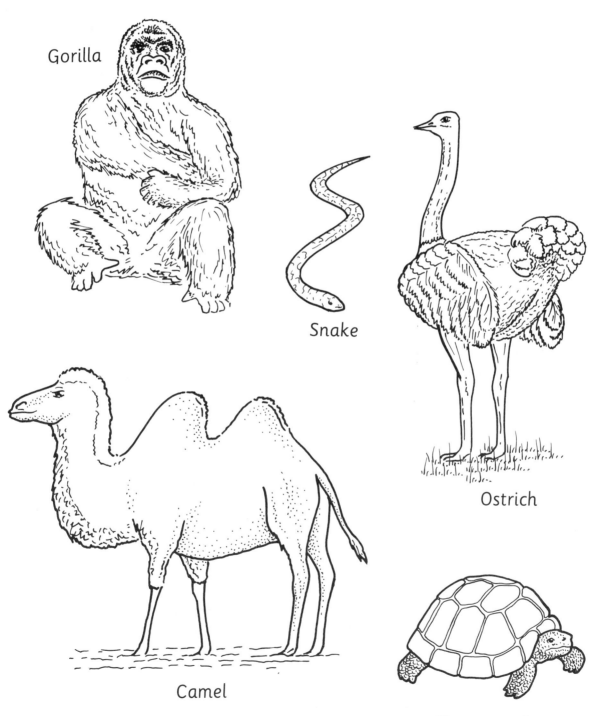

Gorilla

Snake

Ostrich

Camel

Giant tortoise

Badger

Fox

Tawny owl

Mole

Rabbit

Squirrel

Pheasant

Adder

Frog

Deer

Swan

Copymaster 74

Triceratops

Allosaurus

Brachiosaurus

Pteranodon

Diplodocus

Stegosaurus

Fossils

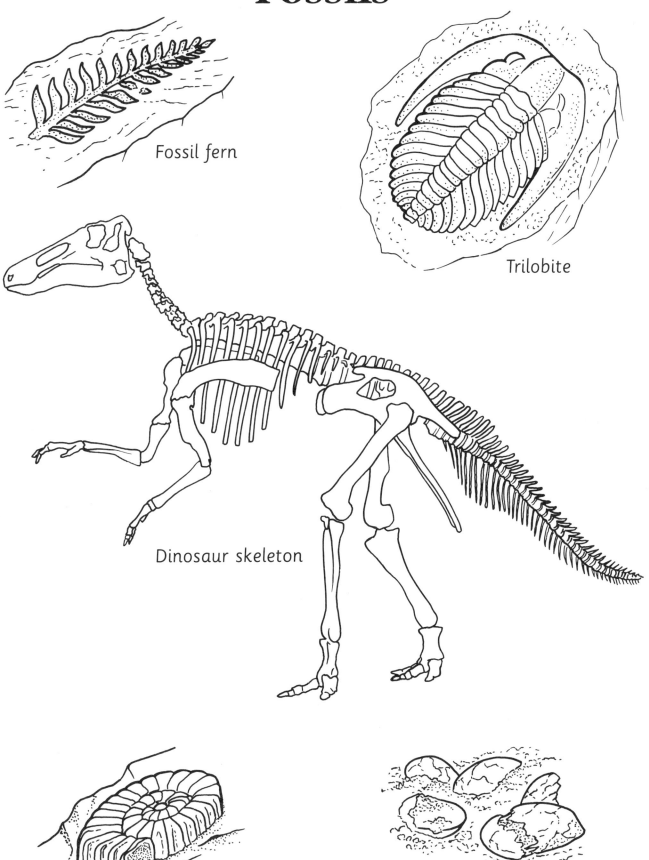

Fossil fern

Trilobite

Dinosaur skeleton

Ammonite

Fossilised eggs

Parts of a flower

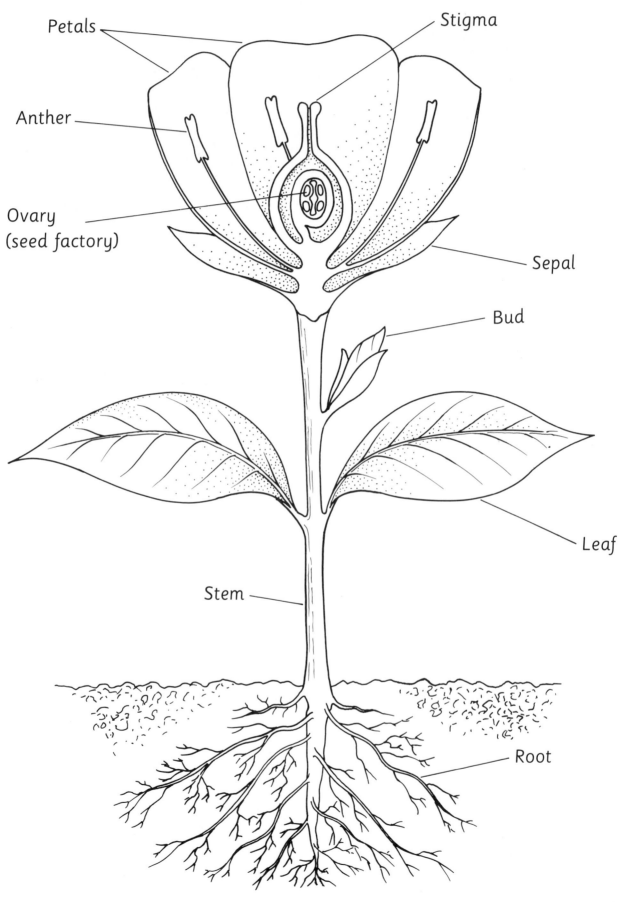

Petals

Stigma

Anther

Ovary
(seed factory)

Sepal

Bud

Leaf

Stem

Root

The human skeleton

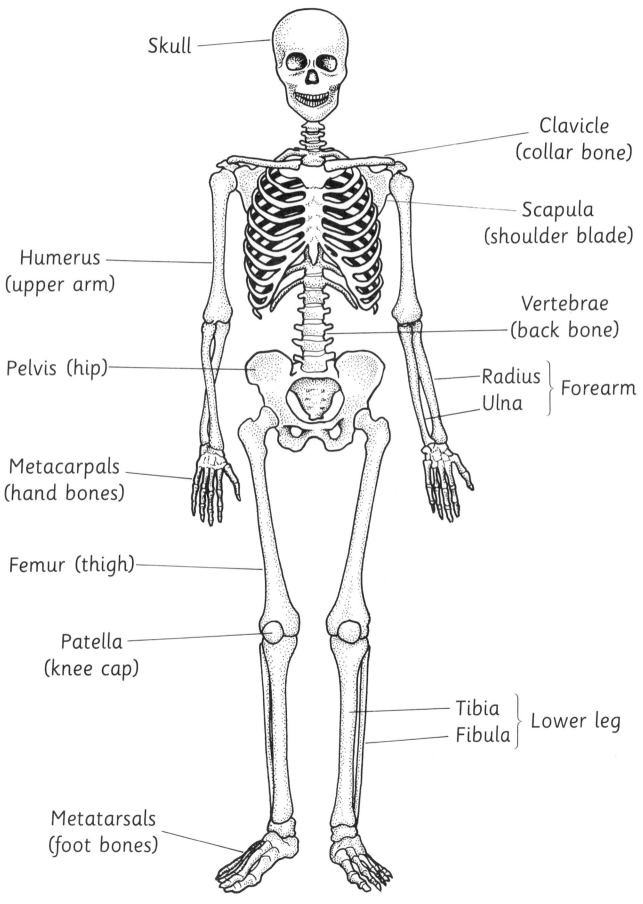

Skull

Clavicle
(collar bone)

Scapula
(shoulder blade)

Humerus
(upper arm)

Vertebrae
(back bone)

Radius
Ulna
} Forearm

Pelvis (hip)

Metacarpals
(hand bones)

Femur (thigh)

Patella
(knee cap)

Tibia
Fibula
} Lower leg

Metatarsals
(foot bones)

The digestive system

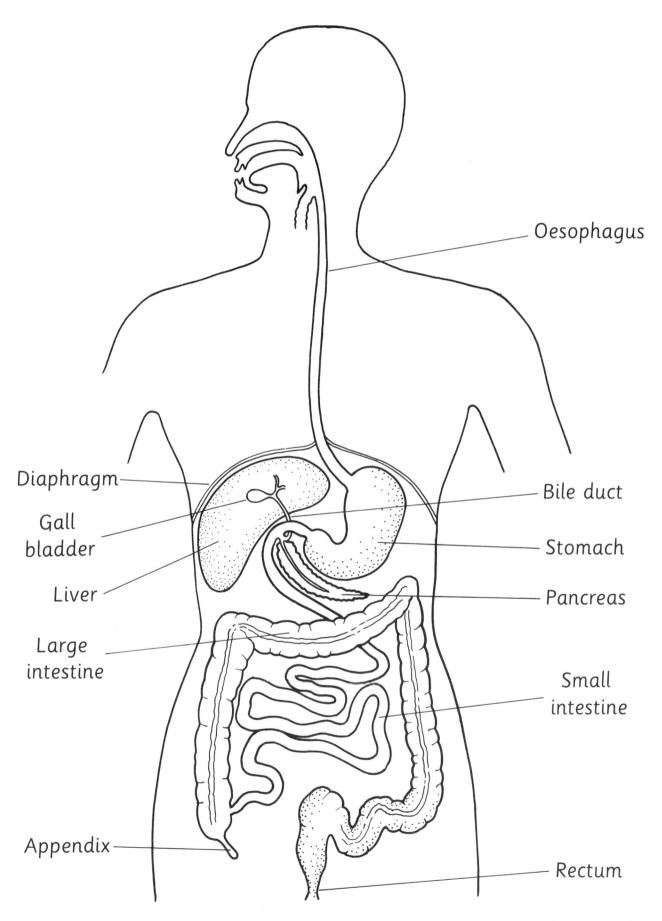

Oesophagus

Diaphragm

Gall
bladder

Liver

Large
intestine

Appendix

Bile duct

Stomach

Pancreas

Small
intestine

Rectum

Inside the ear

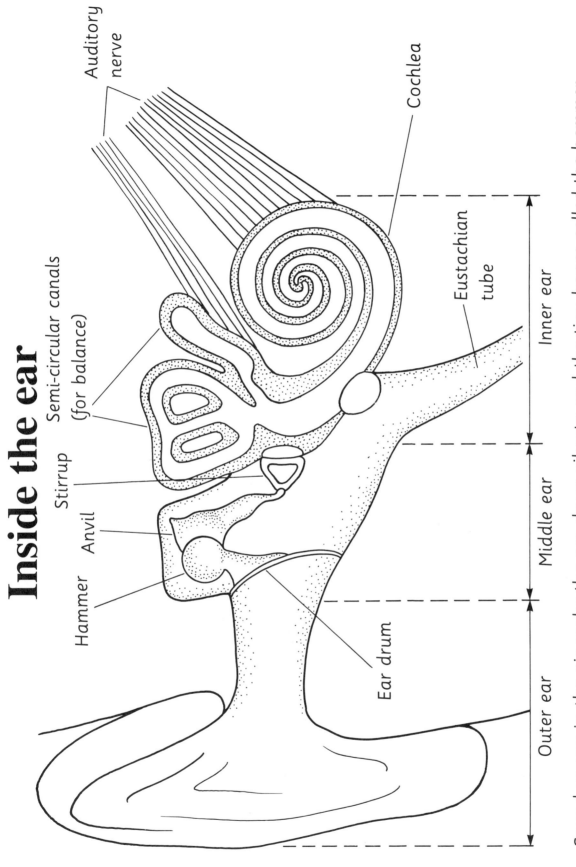

Auditory nerve

Semi-circular canals (for balance)

Stirrup

Anvil

Hammer

Cochlea

Eustachian tube

Ear drum

Inner ear

Middle ear

Outer ear

Sound waves in the air make the ear drum vibrate and the tiny bones called the hammer, anvil and stirrup pass on the vibrations to the inner ear. There (inside the cochlea) the vibrations are converted to electrical impulses that travel to the brain.

The eye

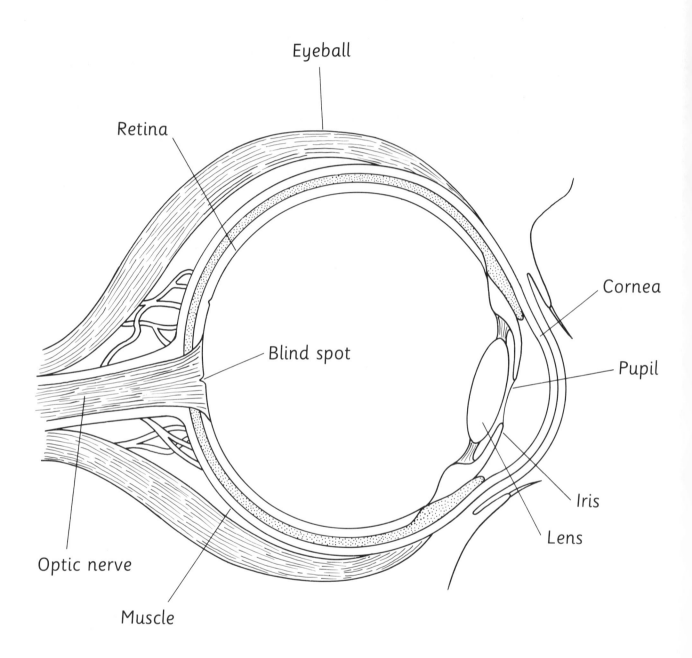

Eyeball

Retina

Blind spot

Cornea

Pupil

Iris

Lens

Optic nerve

Muscle

Swan (pen) and cygnet

Rabbit (doe) and kit or kitten

Giraffe (cow) and calf

Chicken (hen) and chick

Deer (doe) and fawn

Goose and gosling

Dog (bitch) and puppy

Cat (queen) and kitten

Copymaster 83

Owl and owlet

Fox (vixen) and pup or cub

Pig (sow) and piglet

Sheep (ewe) and lamb

Horse (mare) and foal

Bear and cub

Elephant and calf

Lion and cub

Animal homes 1

Squirrels and drey

Foxes and den

Rookery and rooks

Rabbits and warren

Badger and sett

Animal homes 2

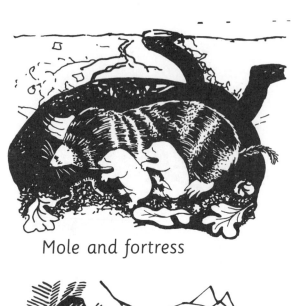

Mole and fortress

Eagle and eyrie

Wolf and lair

Stickleback and nest

Otter and holt

Life cycle of a butterfly

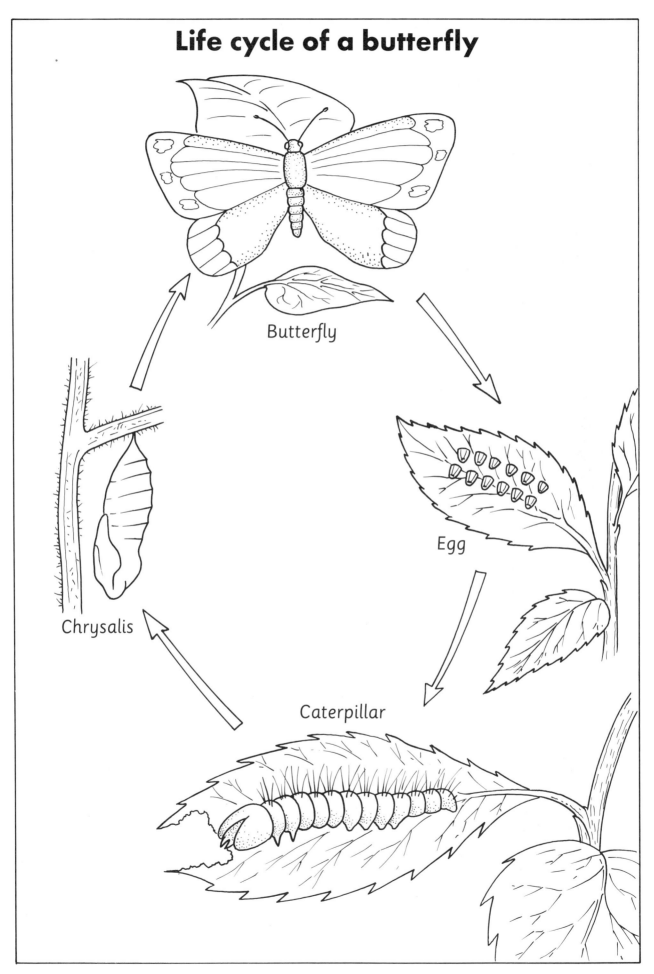

Butterfly

Chrysalis

Egg

Caterpillar

Life cycle of a frog

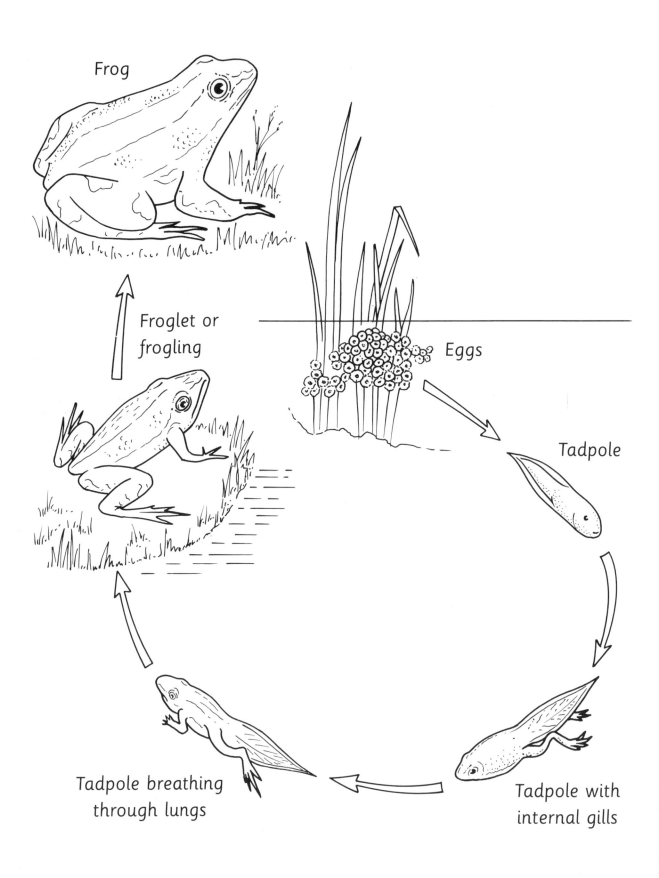

Frog

Froglet or
frogling

Eggs

Tadpole

Tadpole breathing
through lungs

Tadpole with
internal gills

Life cycle of a human

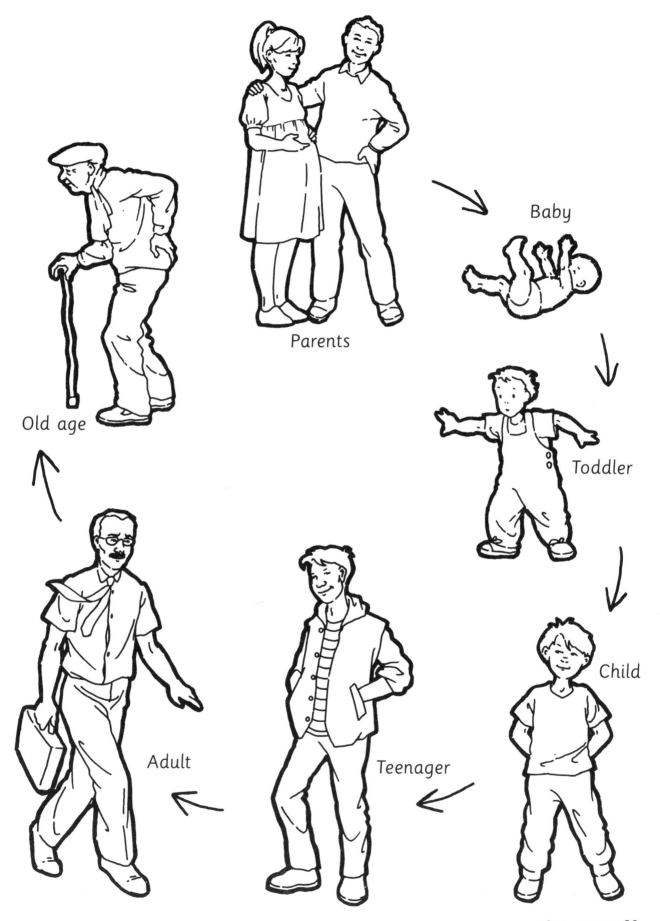

Parents

Baby

Toddler

Child

Teenager

Adult

Old age

Earth in space

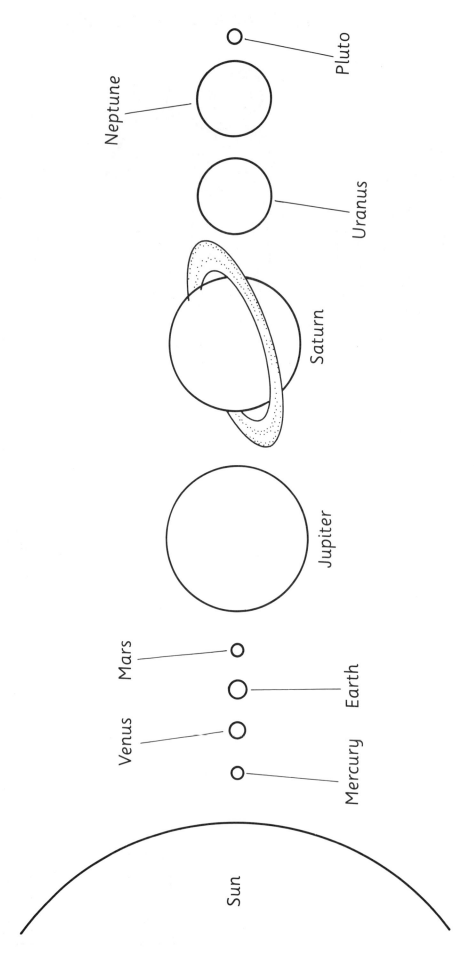

Sun

Mercury

Venus

Earth

Mars

Jupiter

Saturn

Uranus

Neptune

Pluto

Generating electricity

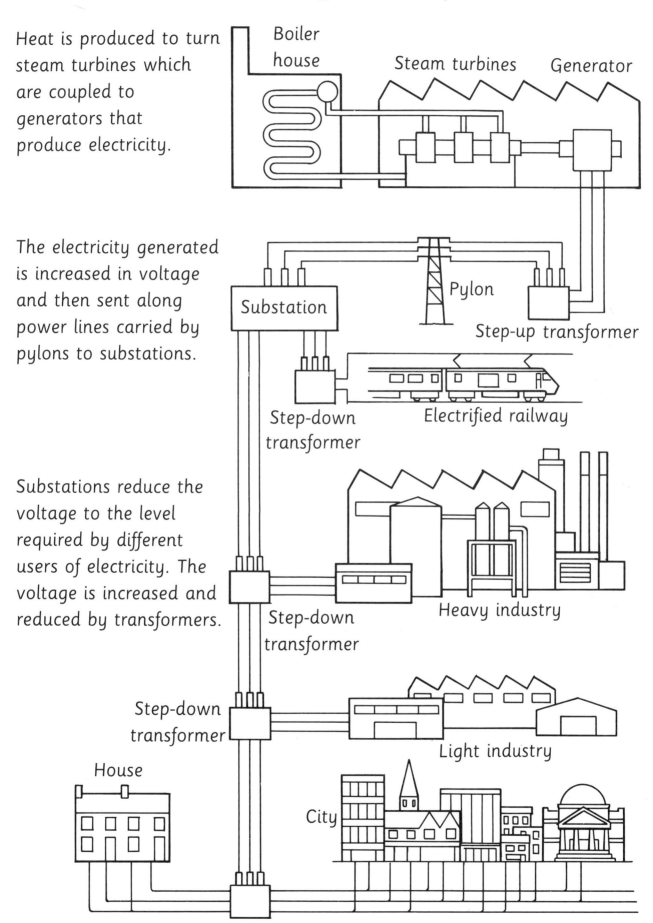

Heat is produced to turn steam turbines which are coupled to generators that produce electricity.

Boiler house

Steam turbines

Generator

The electricity generated is increased in voltage and then sent along power lines carried by pylons to substations.

Substation

Pylon

Step-up transformer

Step-down transformer

Electrified railway

Substations reduce the voltage to the level required by different users of electricity. The voltage is increased and reduced by transformers.

Step-down transformer

Heavy industry

Step-down transformer

Light industry

House

City

How a steam engine works

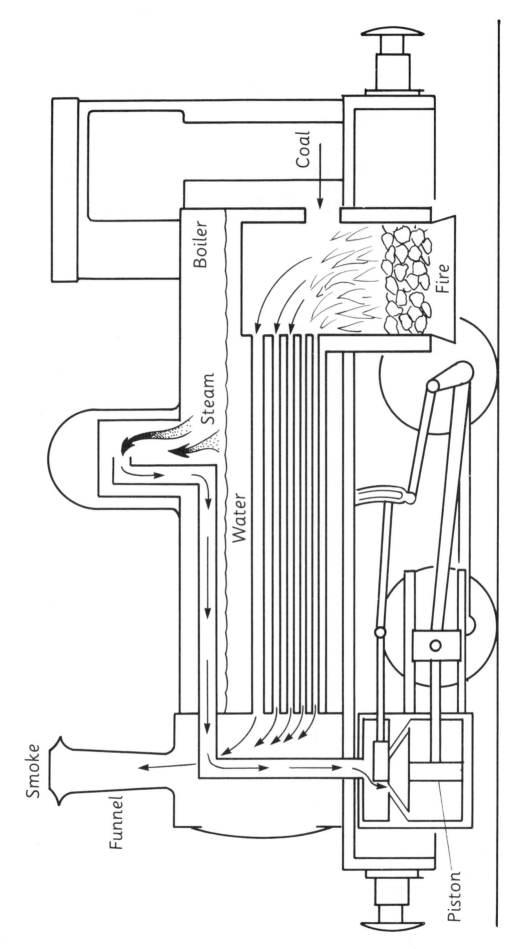

Smoke

Funnel

Boiler

Coal

Steam

Water

Fire

Piston

In a steam engine, steam is made by heating water in a boiler. The steam pushes the pistons backwards and forwards and this turns the wheels.

Motorcycle and bicycle

Motorcycle

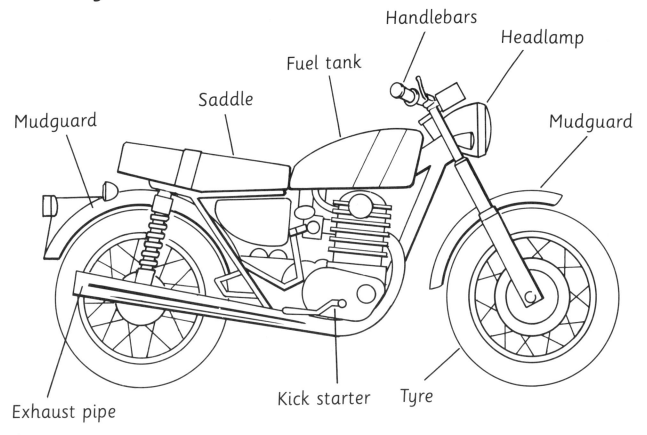

Handlebars

Headlamp

Fuel tank

Saddle

Mudguard

Mudguard

Exhaust pipe

Kick starter

Tyre

Bicycle

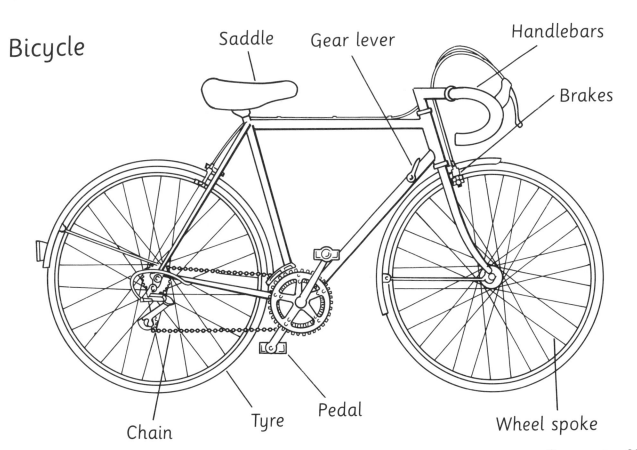

Saddle

Gear lever

Handlebars

Brakes

Chain

Tyre

Pedal

Wheel spoke

Space vehicles

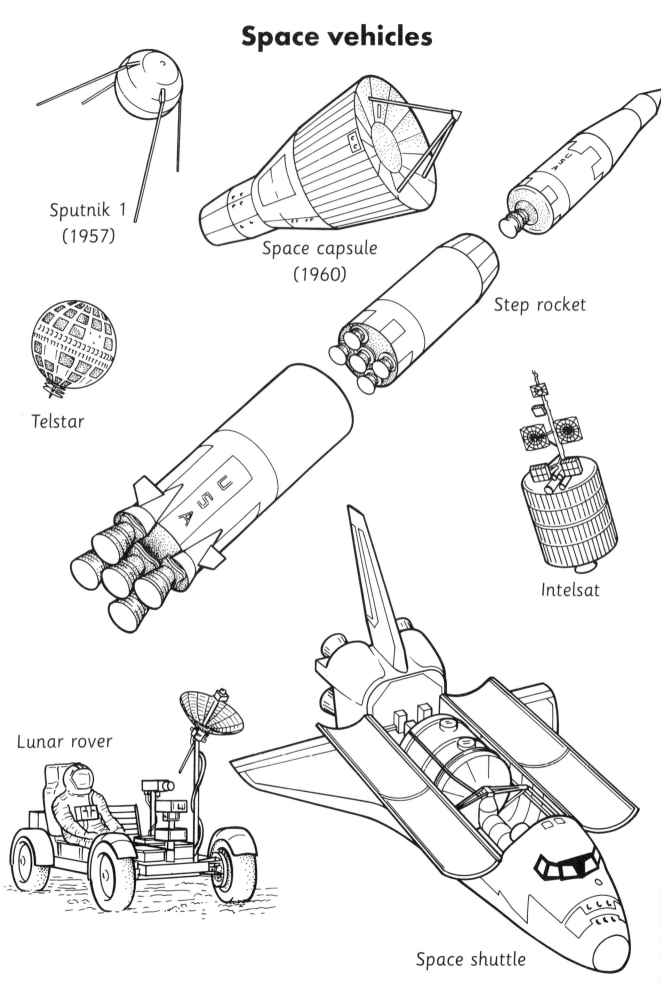

Sputnik 1
(1957)

Space capsule
(1960)

Step rocket

Telstar

Intelsat

Lunar rover

Space shuttle

Bridges

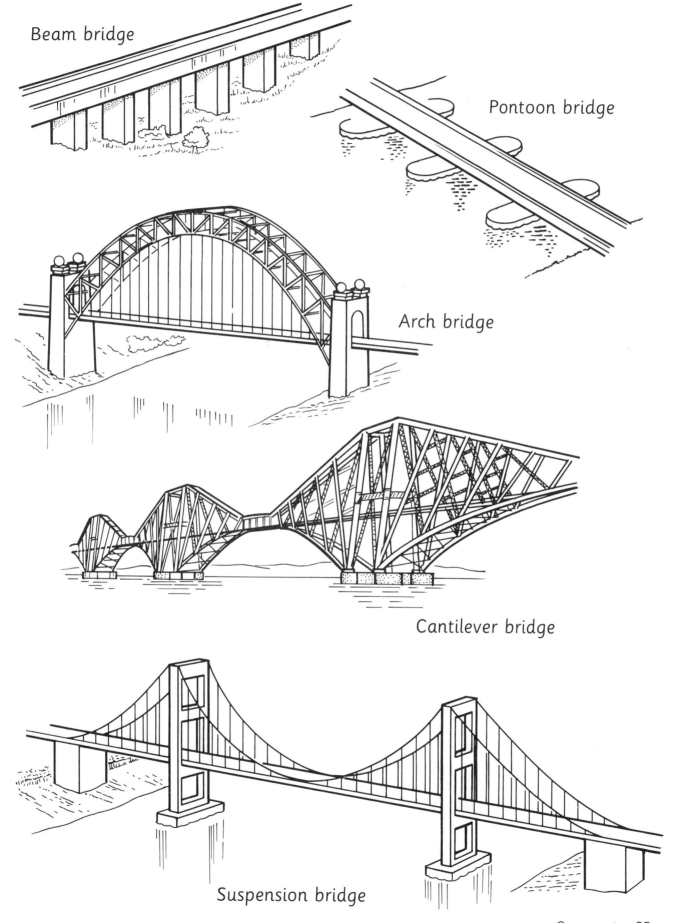

Beam bridge

Pontoon bridge

Arch bridge

Cantilever bridge

Suspension bridge

Food chains

Food chain in a field

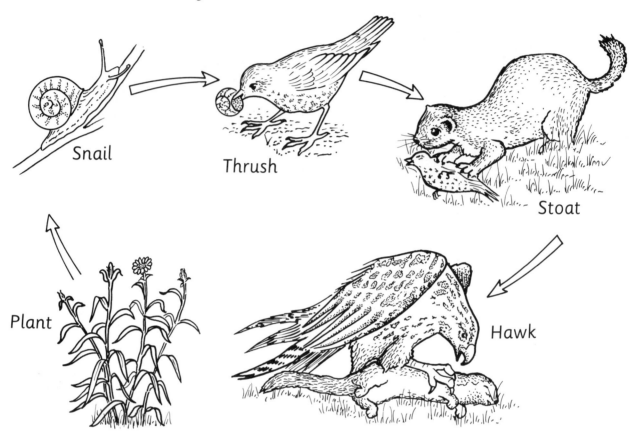

Snail

Thrush

Stoat

Plant

Hawk

Food chain in the sea

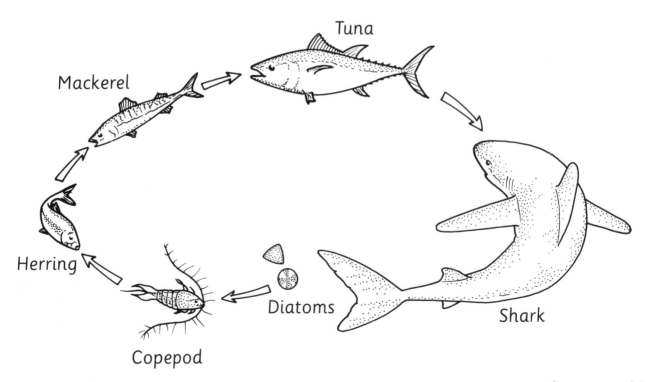

Tuna

Mackerel

Herring

Diatoms

Copepod

Shark

Landforms

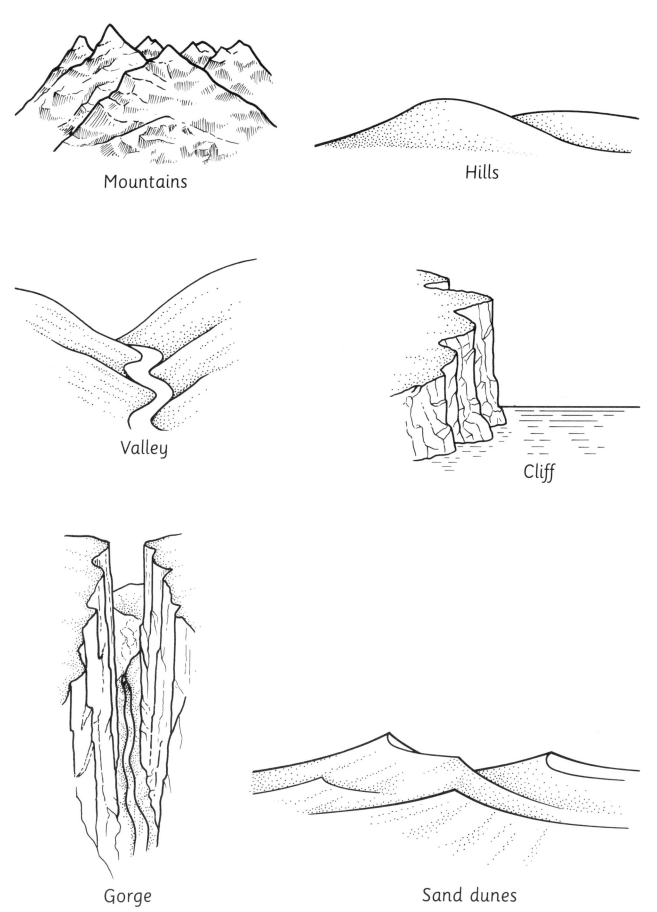

Mountains

Hills

Valley

Cliff

Gorge

Sand dunes

Habitats

Jungle

Desert

Bog or marsh

Woodland

Polar regions

Grasslands

Transport 1 (sea)

Transport 2 (land)

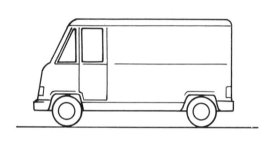

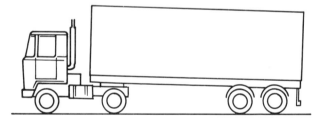

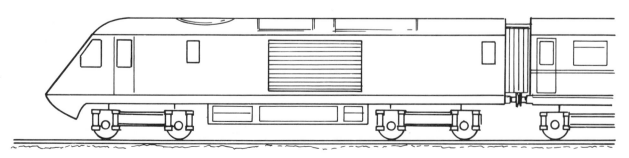

Transport 3 (air)

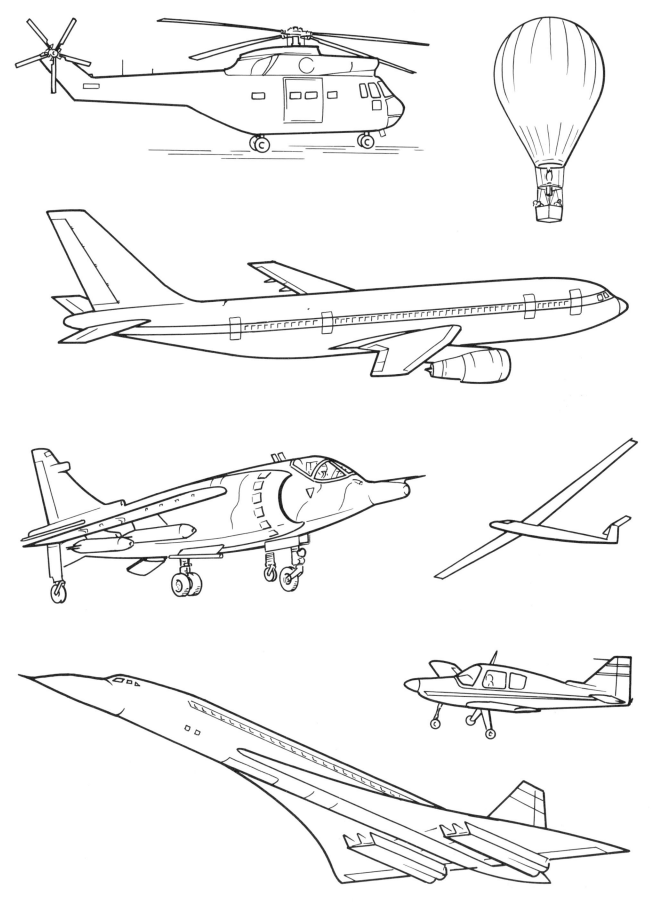

The water cycle

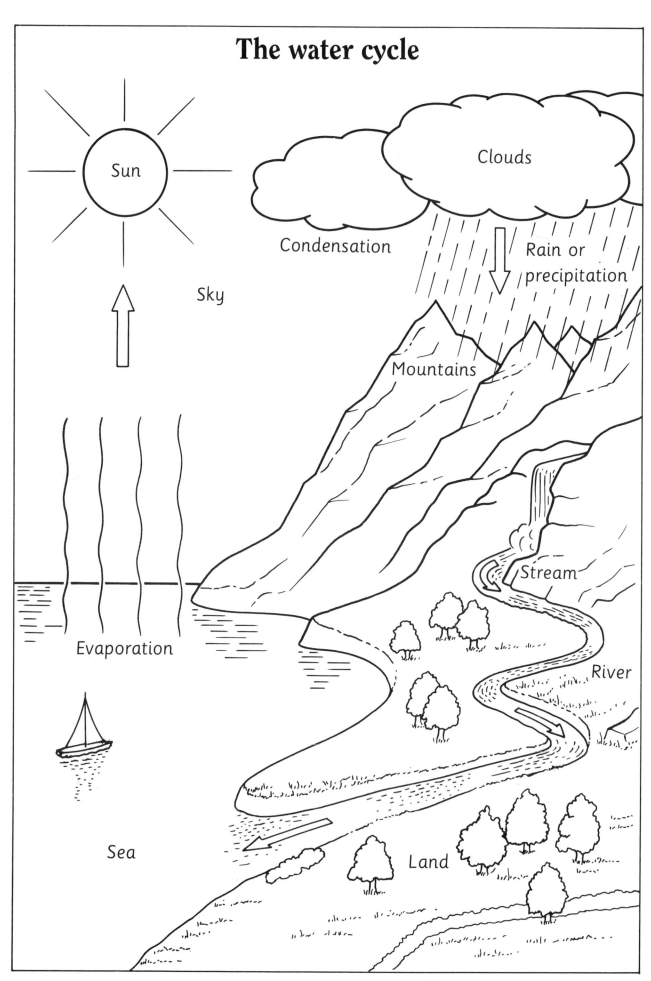

Sun

Clouds

Condensation

Rain or precipitation

Sky

Mountains

Stream

River

Evaporation

Sea

Land

Common trees and their leaves

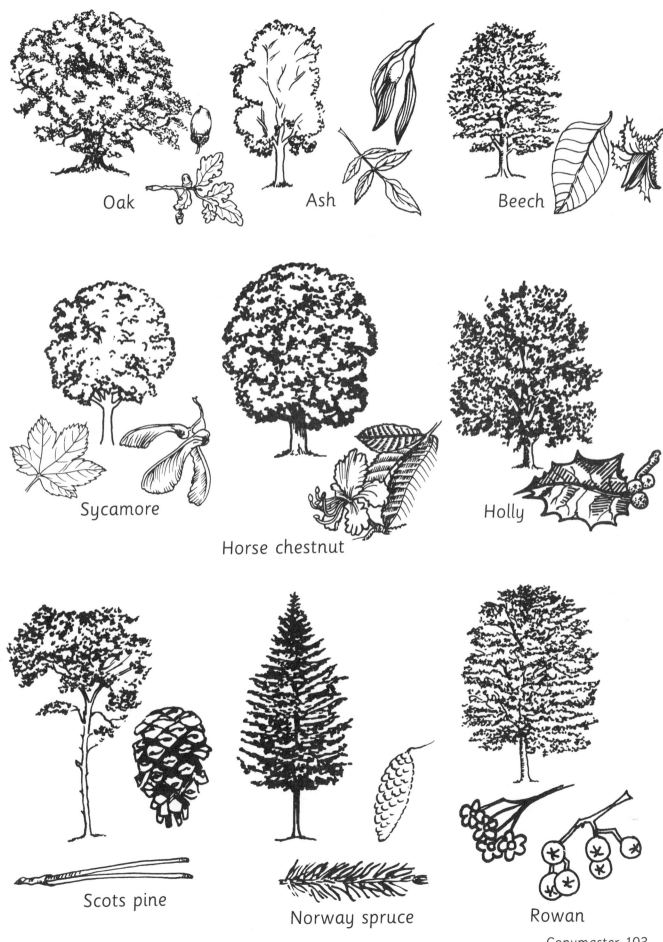

Oak

Ash

Beech

Sycamore

Horse chestnut

Holly

Scots pine

Norway spruce

Rowan

Garden and wild flowers

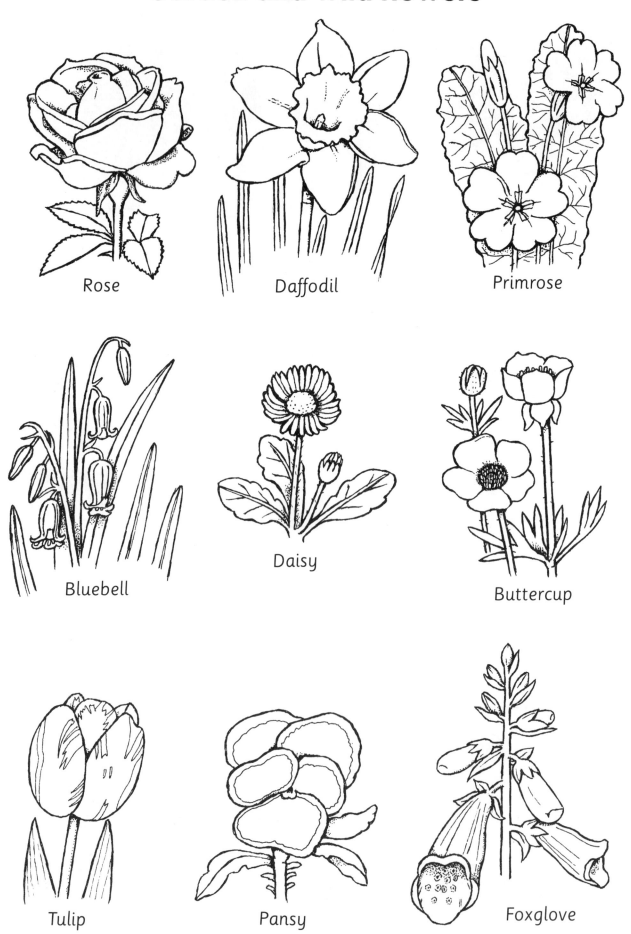

Rose

Daffodil

Primrose

Bluebell

Daisy

Buttercup

Tulip

Pansy

Foxglove

Farm animals

Horse

Cow

Pig

Sheep

Goat

Hen

Duck

Turkey

Cat

Dog

Food

Food from animals

Meat: beef from cattle; lamb and mutton from sheep; ham, bacon and pork from pigs; poultry such as chicken and turkey.

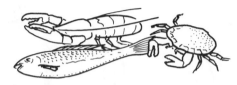

Seafood: fish (including freshwater fish), crab, lobster, prawns, squid and shellfish (oysters, clams, mussels).

Dairyfoods and eggs: milk, butter, cheese, yoghurt and eggs.

Food from plants

Fruit: such as apples, pears, cherries, oranges, grapefruit and bananas.

Vegetables: such as cauliflower, potatoes, peas, carrots and cabbage.

Cereals: such as bread and pasta (from wheat), rice, oats and corn.

Drinks: such as coffee, tea, cocoa, fruit juices and water.

Other foods: such as nuts, vegetable oils, margarine, sugar and syrup.

The orchestra

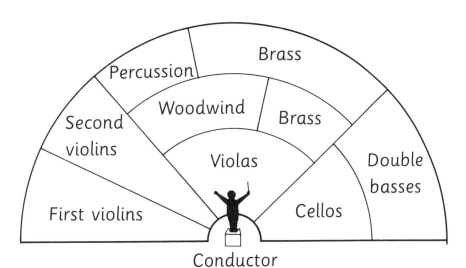

- Brass
- Percussion
- Woodwind
- Brass
- Second violins
- Violas
- Double basses
- First violins
- Cellos
- Conductor

Stringed instruments

Harp
Violin
Cello
Lute
Guitar

Brass instruments

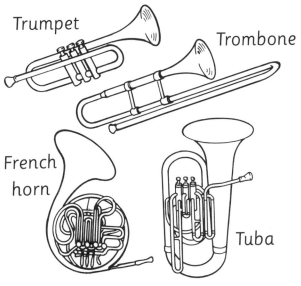

Trumpet
Trombone
French horn
Tuba

Woodwind instruments

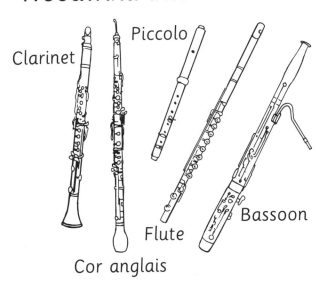

Clarinet
Piccolo
Flute
Bassoon
Cor anglais

Percussion instruments

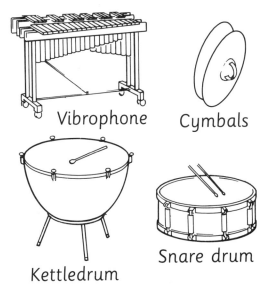

Vibrophone
Cymbals
Kettledrum
Snare drum

Compass points

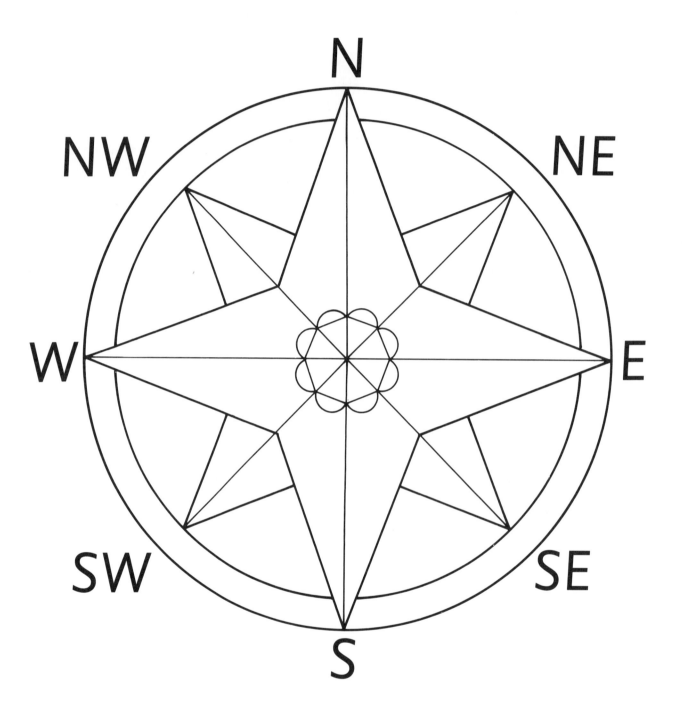

north	south	east	west
northwest		northeast	
southwest		southeast	

British Isles

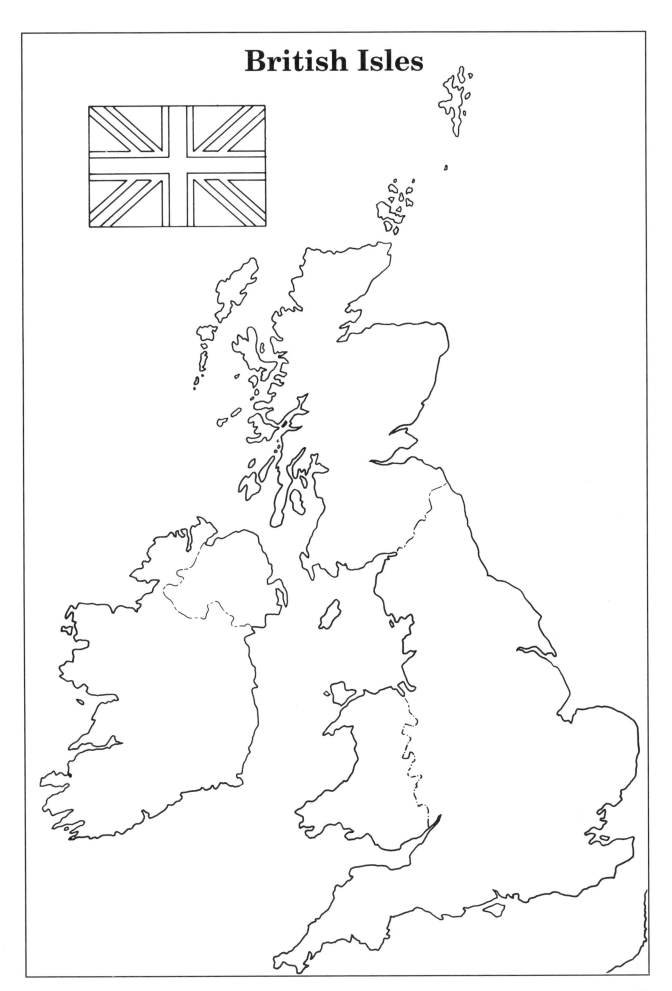

England

Ireland

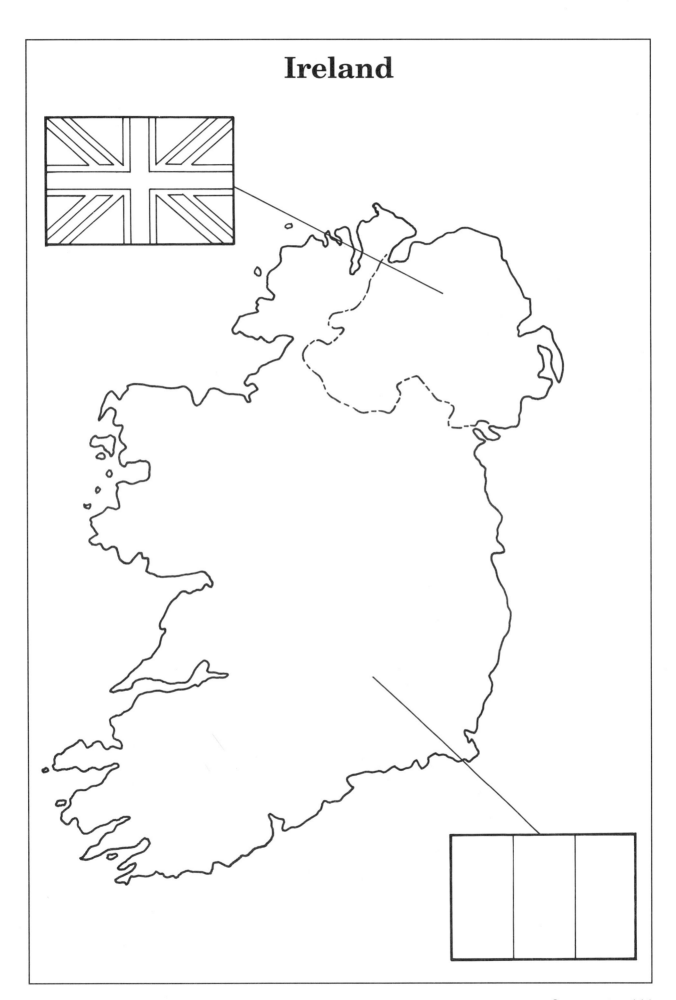

Scotland

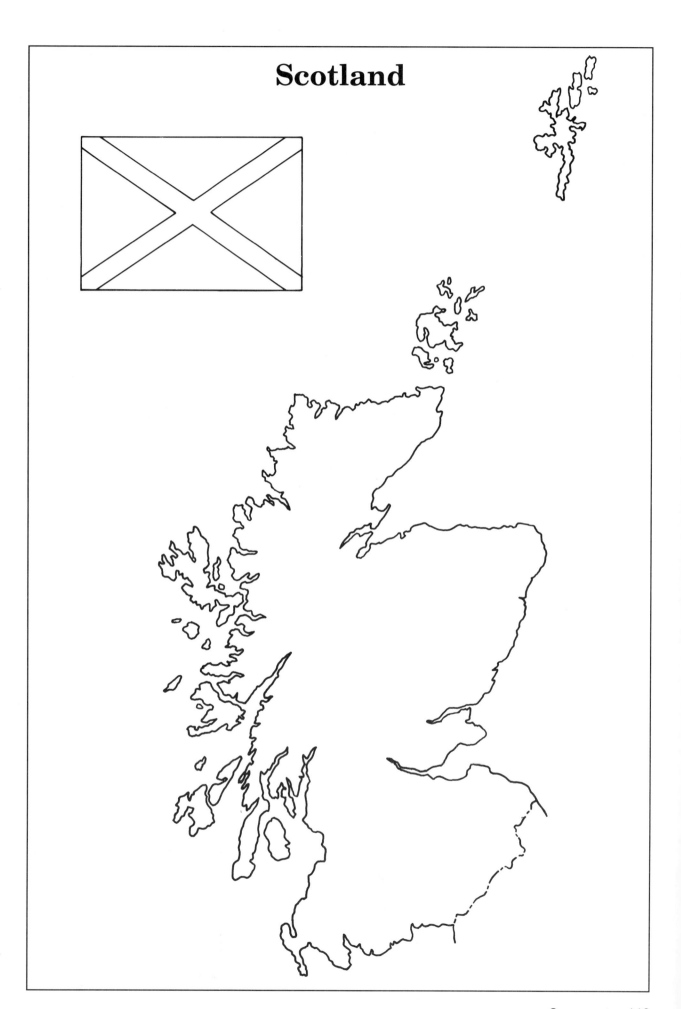

Wales

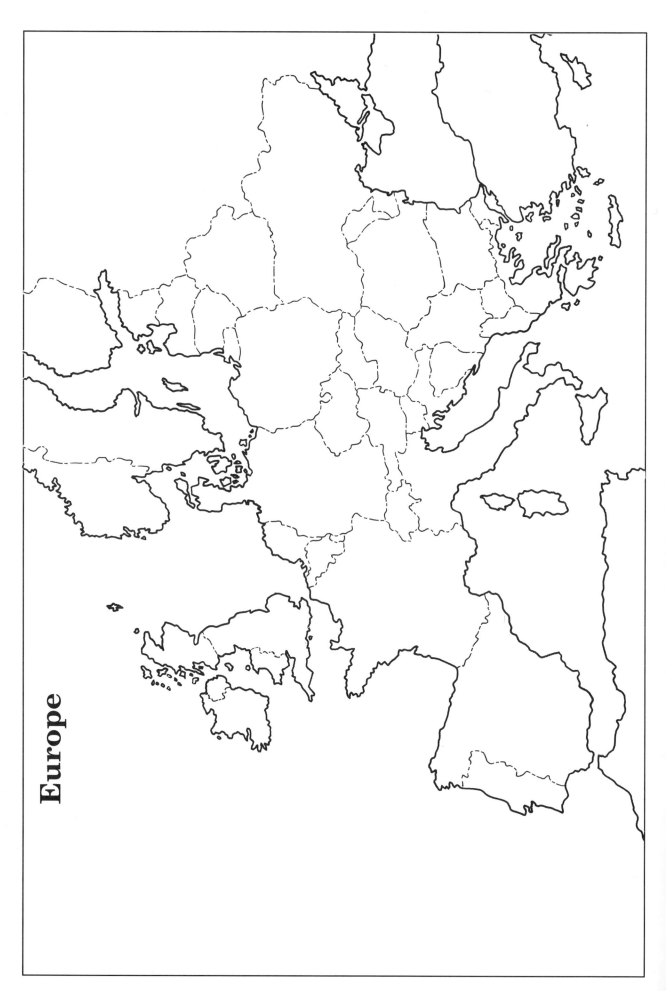

Europe

The world

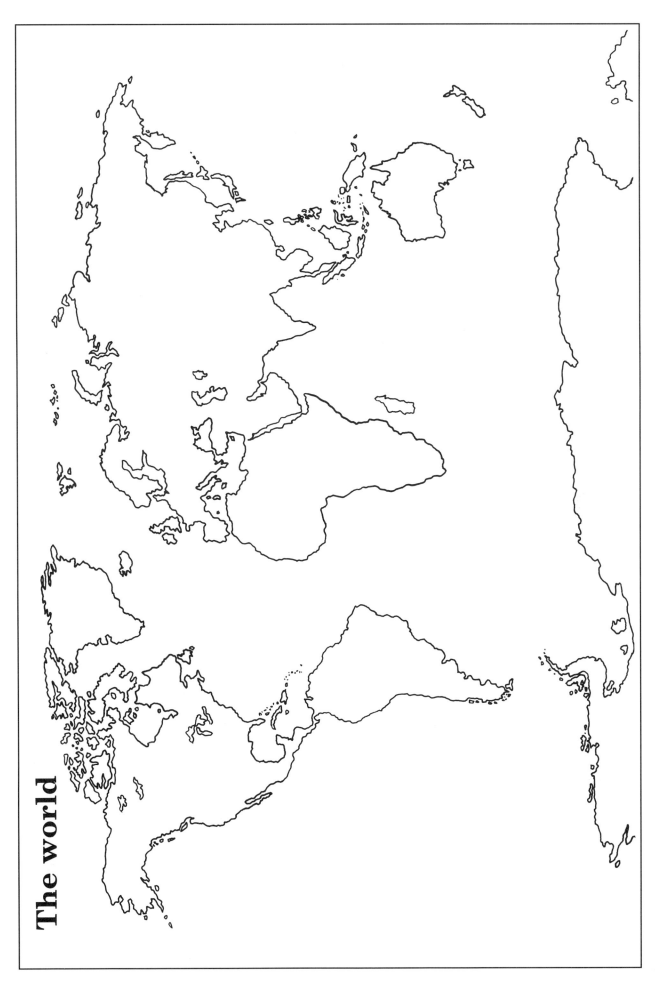

Famous buildings 1

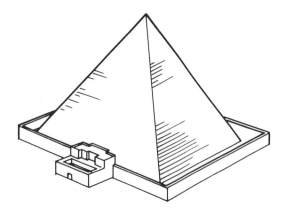

Pyramids of Egypt

Great wall of China

Eiffel Tower

Leaning Tower of Pisa

Statue of Liberty

Taj Mahal

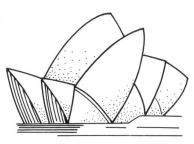

Sydney Opera House

St Peter's, Rome

Famous buildings 2

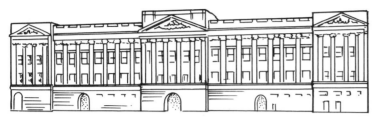
Buckingham Palace

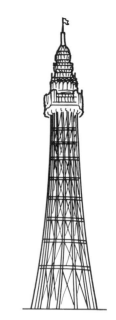
Blackpool Tower

Forth Railway Bridge

York Minster

St Paul's Cathedral

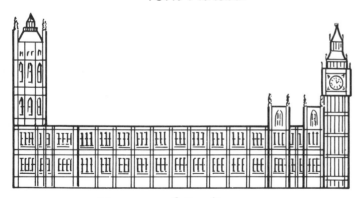
Houses of Parliament

Edinburgh Castle

Caernarfon Castle

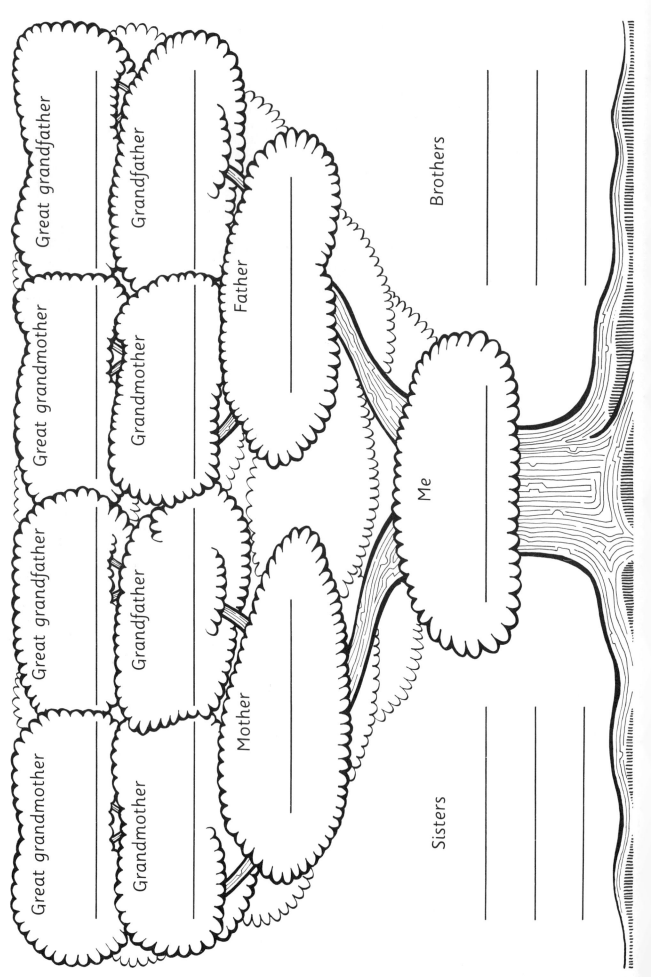

Great grandfather

Great grandmother

Great grandfather

Great grandmother

Grandfather

Grandmother

Grandfather

Grandmother

Father

Mother

Me

Brothers

Sisters

The royal family

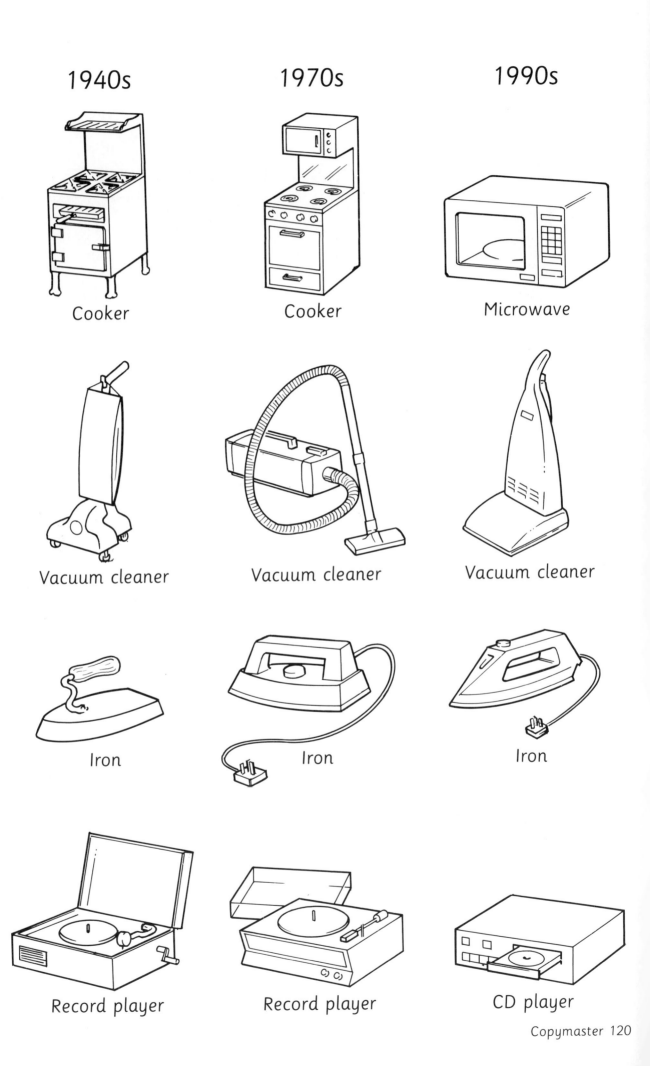

	1940s	1970s	1990s
	Cooker	Cooker	Microwave
	Vacuum cleaner	Vacuum cleaner	Vacuum cleaner
	Iron	Iron	Iron
	Record player	Record player	CD player

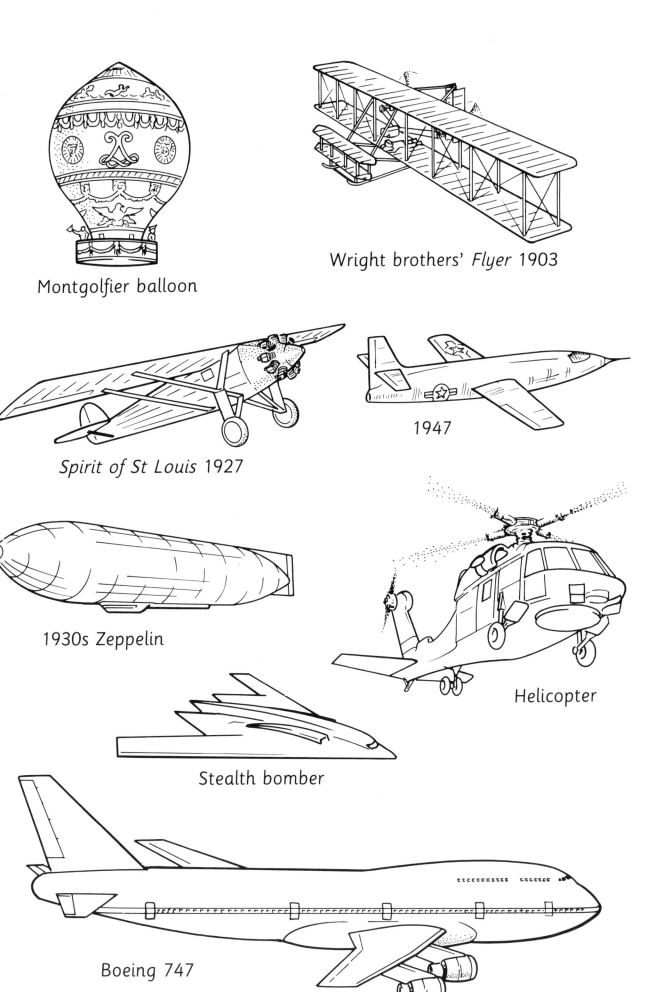

Montgolfier balloon

Wright brothers' *Flyer* 1903

Spirit of St Louis 1927

1947

1930s Zeppelin

Helicopter

Stealth bomber

Boeing 747

Viking longship

Greek galley

16th century galleon

Clipper 1820

Paddle steamer 1858

Battleship 1940

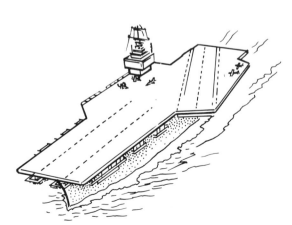

Aircraft carrier

Double-hulled catamaran

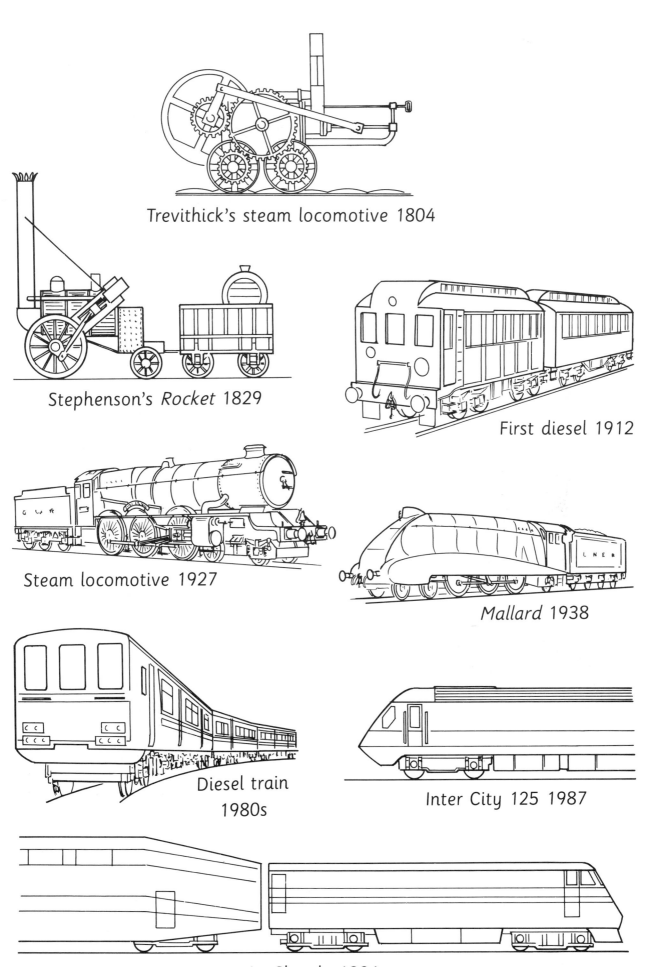

Trevithick's steam locomotive 1804

Stephenson's *Rocket* 1829

First diesel 1912

Steam locomotive 1927

Mallard 1938

Diesel train
1980s

Inter City 125 1987

Le Shuttle 1994

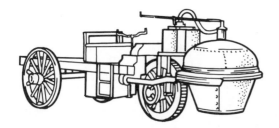

Cugnot's steam gun carriage 1770

Karl Benz's first car 1885

Rolls-Royce Silver Ghost 1911

Ford Model T 1908–1927

Citroen Traction Avant 1934

Volkswagen 'Beetle' 1939

Lincoln Continental Cabriolet 1947

Austin Mini 1959

Range Rover Vogue 1988

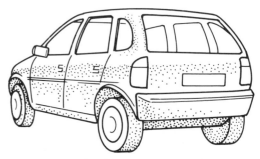

Vauxhall Corsa 1994

1940s

1960s

1990s

Homes time line 1

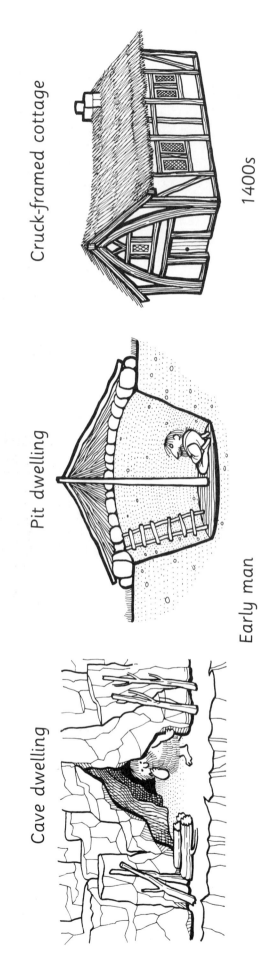

Cave dwelling

Pit dwelling

Early man

Cruck-framed cottage

1400s

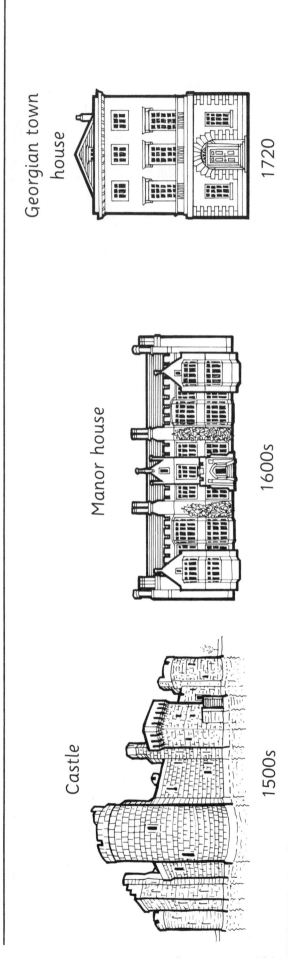

Castle

1500s

Manor house

1600s

Georgian town house

1720

Homes time line 2

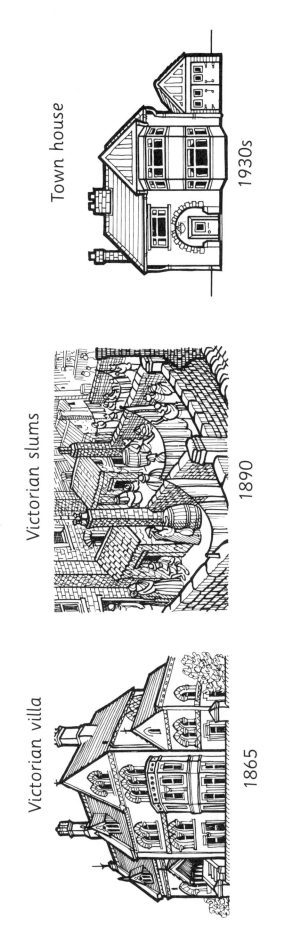

Victorian villa
1865

Victorian slums
1890

Town house
1930s

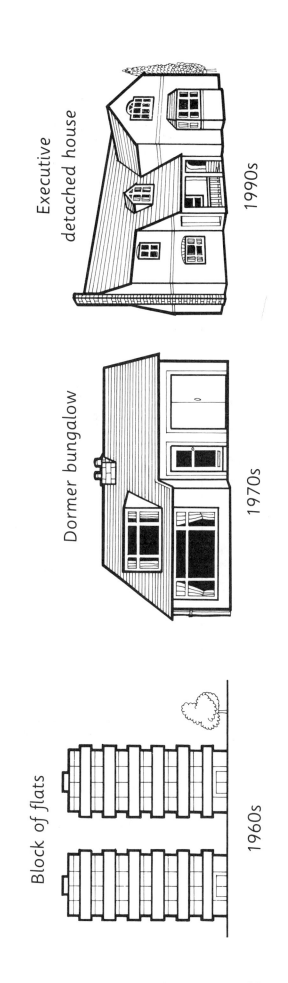

Block of flats
1960s

Dormer bungalow
1970s

Executive detached house
1990s

Toys time line 1

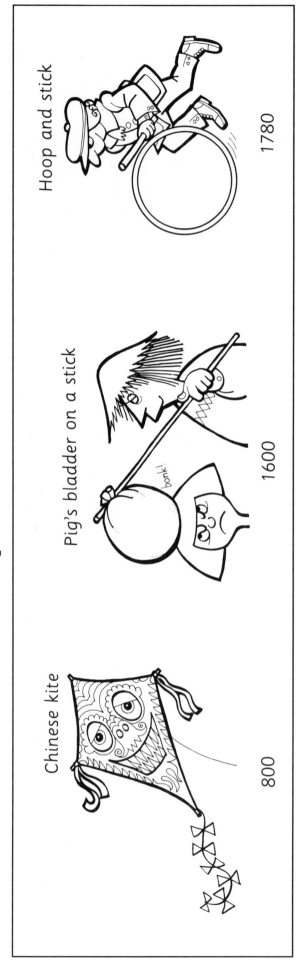

Chinese kite — 800

Pig's bladder on a stick — 1600

Hoop and stick — 1780

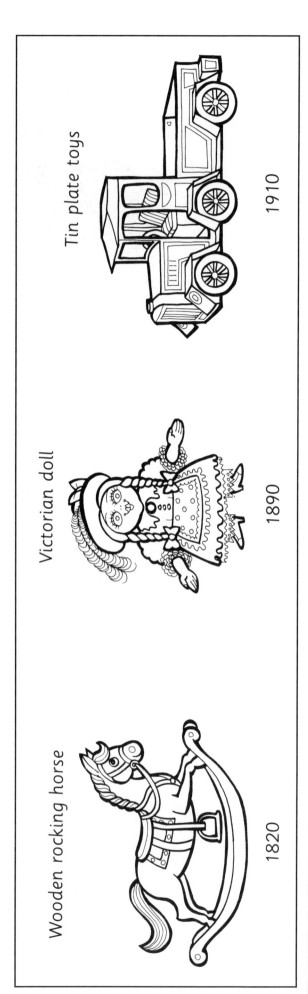

Wooden rocking horse — 1820

Victorian doll — 1890

Tin plate toys — 1910

Toys time line 2

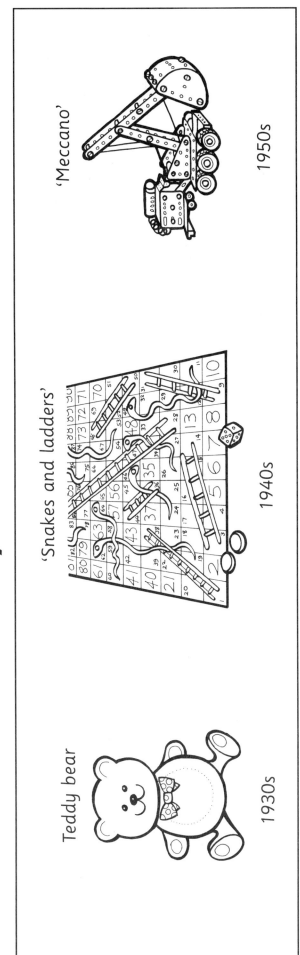

Teddy bear

1930s

'Snakes and ladders'

1940s

'Meccano'

1950s

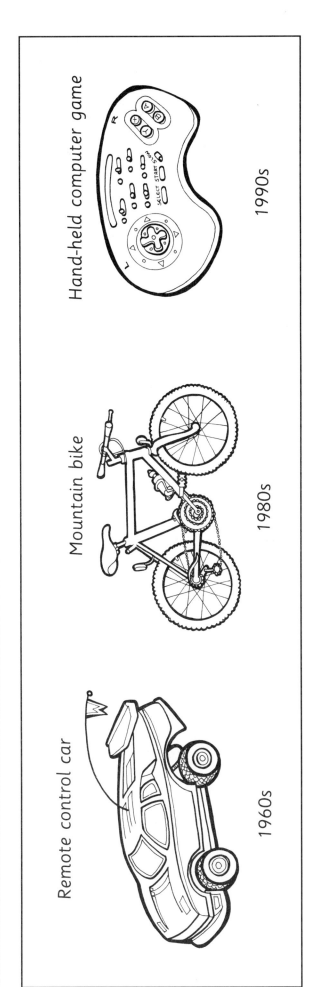

Remote control car

1960s

Mountain bike

1980s

Hand-held computer game

1990s

Julius Caesar

Cleopatra

Henry VIII

Queen
Elizabeth I

Galileo

Joan of Arc

Florence
Nightingale

Newton

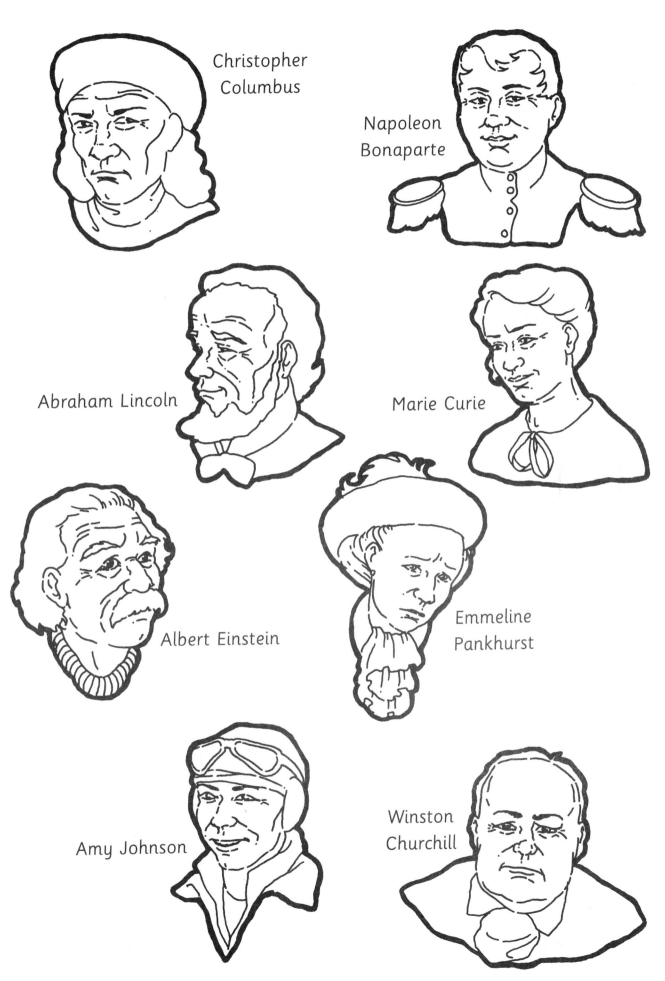

Christopher Columbus

Napoleon Bonaparte

Abraham Lincoln

Marie Curie

Albert Einstein

Emmeline Pankhurst

Amy Johnson

Winston Churchill

16th century galleon

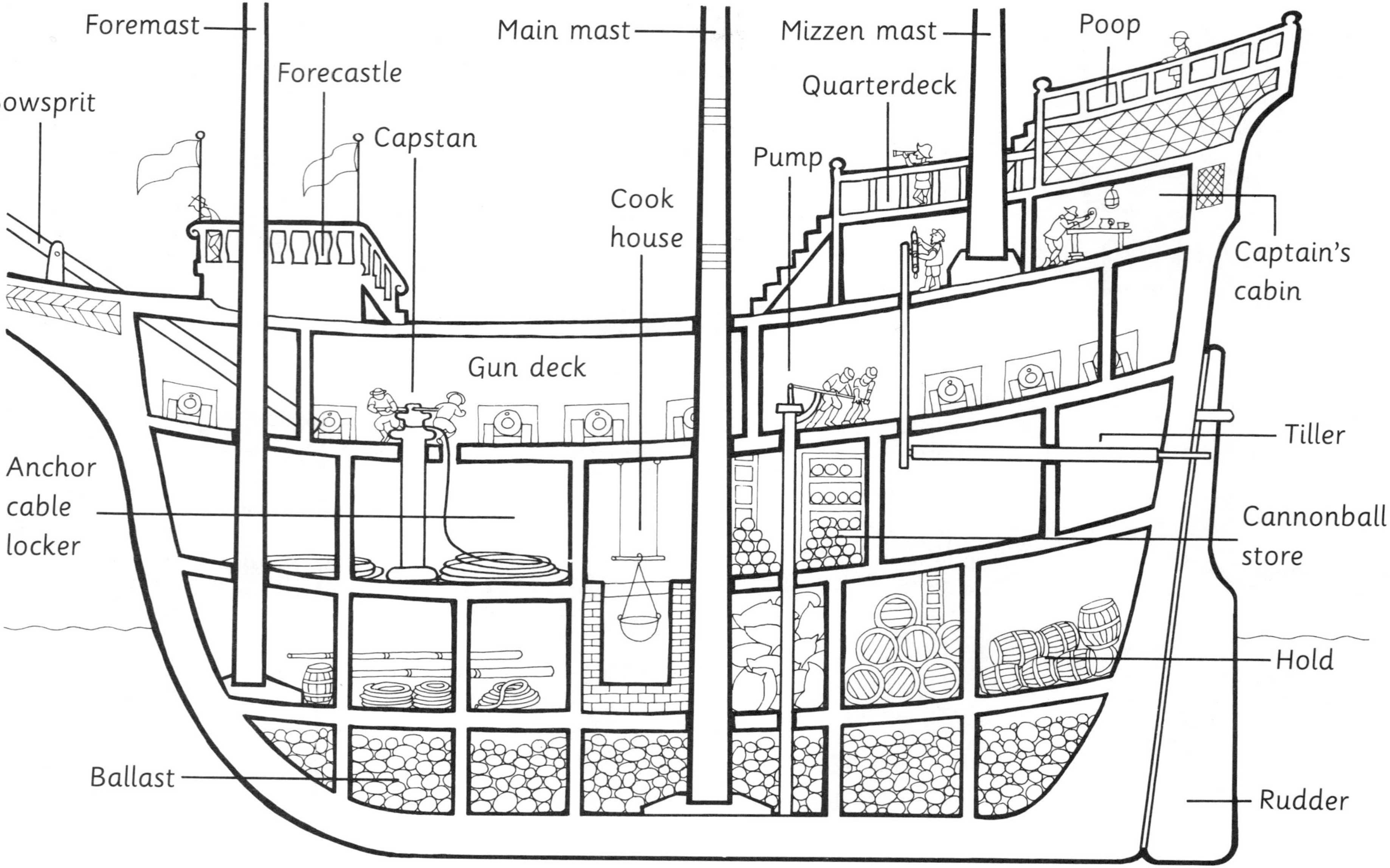

Foremast

Bowsprit

Forecastle

Capstan

Main mast

Cook house

Gun deck

Anchor cable locker

Ballast

Mizzen mast

Quarterdeck

Pump

Poop

Captain's cabin

Tiller

Cannonball store

Hold

Rudder

Roman town in Britain

Anglo Saxon village

Viking settlement

Castle life

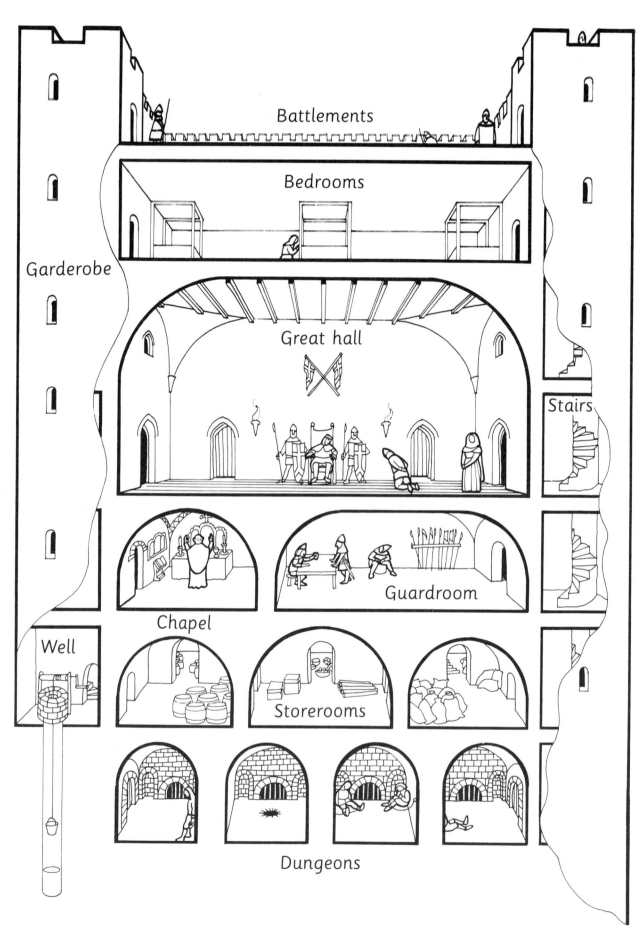

Battlements

Bedrooms

Garderobe

Great hall

Stairs

Chapel

Guardroom

Well

Storerooms

Dungeons

Georgian town

Victorian farm

Victorian town

M.J.BENSON CORN CHANDLERS

MOSSOP · BOOTMAKER

Life in the 1920s

Life in the 1990s

A note from your teacher

A note from your teacher

Special event

Special Award for Working Hard

Awarded to

Special Award for Punctuality

Awarded to

Special Award for Good Manners

Awarded to

Special Award for Helping Hand

Awarded to

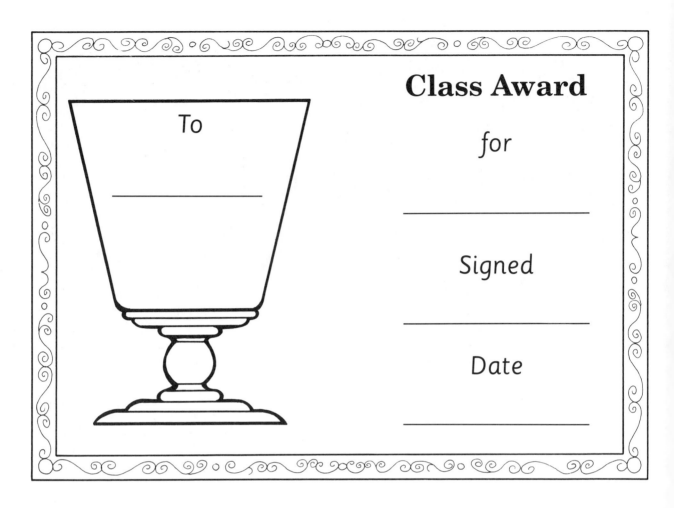

Class Award

To

for

_____

Signed

_____

Date

_____

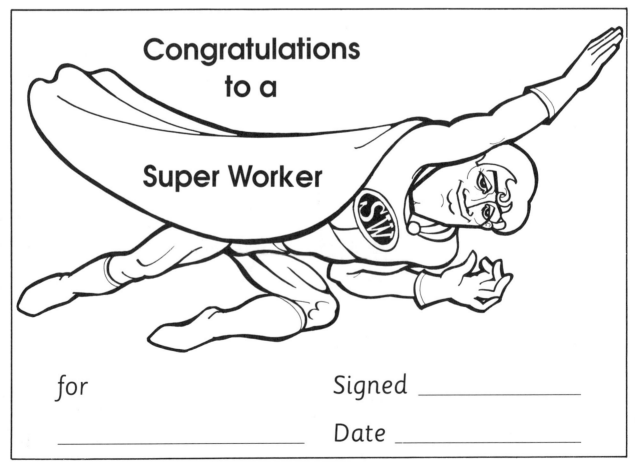

Congratulations
to a

Super Worker

for

_____

Signed _____

Date _____

Sports Award

This is to certify that

_____

_____

Signed _____ Date _____

This is to certify that

_____

is a

Super Reader

Signed _____

Date _____

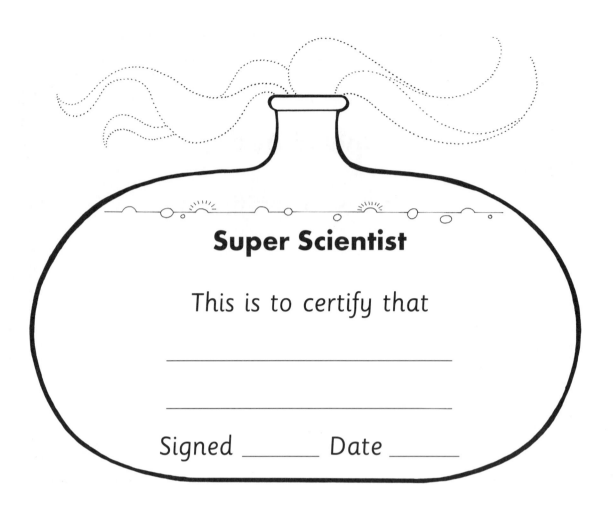

Super Scientist

This is to certify that

_____

_____

Signed _____ Date _____

This is to certify that

_____

is a

Computer Expert

Signed _____ Date _____

Handwriting Expert

This is to certify that

_____

_____

Signed _____ Date _____

Maths Award

This is to certify that

_____

_____

Signed _____ Date _____

Border text: 0 + 7,231,590·338 ÷ 12 + ³⁄₁₆ × 405 − 7,231,590·338 ÷ 12 + ³⁄₁₆ × 405 = 0 1,789 + 10 ÷ 55 × 2 ÷ 4 = 64 1,789 + 20 ÷ 64 × 55 0

For making good music

This is to certify that

_____

_____

Signed _____ Date _____

Super Painter

This is to certify that

_____

_____

Signed _____

Date _____